GROWING UP IN LEE-ON-THE-SOLENT

GROWING UP IN LEE-ON-THE-SOLENT

John W Green

CHAPLIN BOOKS

www.chaplinbooks.co.uk

First published in 2014 by Chaplin Books

ISBN 978-1-909183-62-9

A CIP catalogue record for this book is available from The British Library.

Design by Michael Walsh at The Better Book Company
Printed by Imprint Digital

Chaplin Books
1 Eliza Place
Gosport PO12 4UN
Tel: 023 9252 9020
www.chaplinbooks.co.uk

In memory of
Robin A Money
1956-2013

Also by John W Green:

Exploring the History of Lee-on-the-Solent
(with Robin A Money)

CONTENTS

1

A VISION OF BEAUTY

It was that day – the embarrassing one, the one when the father takes his son to one side and talks to him 'man to man' about the facts of life. '*Well son, you're going out into the big wide world and in places like London there are women who will get money from you by other means than robbing you, so take care.*'

This was the day that I was leaving to join the RAF as a Radio Fitter Apprentice. So much for the sex education! It was not as descriptive or lurid as the version given to me by the older boys of the various groups that I had been knocking about with for the last few years. '*Right Dad,*' I replied. He gave me a pat on the shoulder and that was that.

Those past few months had been a period of reassessment, one of those times in life when fate unexpectedly dictates events. It was the summer of 1949, and I had taken my School Certificate the previous year, but to my utter surprise, against all expectations, and to my parents' disappointment, I had failed. I had passed in seven out of nine subjects, with two distinctions, four credits and a single pass, but I had failed English Literature and – more importantly – I had failed English Language. A good performance in the other subjects counted for nothing: without a pass in English Language, the School Certificate was not awarded.

As a consequence of this failure, I could not progress to the sixth form and ended up in an educational limbo for the first term of the new educational year. Instead of attending Lower Sixth lessons, I had to prepare for the re-sits which would take place in the December and then, unlike today, *all* subjects had to be retaken.

The re-sits were held in the Municipal College building which was situated behind Portsmouth Guildhall. Later the 'Muni' became a 'Poly' until its eventual elevation to University status. Together with the other re-sit candidates from schools across Portsmouth and the surrounding area, I entered the foyer of the imposing Victorian edifice to be directed to the rooms where the exams were to be taken. Initially, the size of some of the rooms was quite daunting. The re-sit exam that I remember most vividly was 'object drawing', which was part of the Art exam. I was a pupil at St John's College in Southsea, which was a single-sex school. Schools were known as 'mixed' or 'all-girl' or 'all-boy' schools, avoiding that awkward 'sex' word. I found all the re-sit exams to be quite exciting because they were held in rooms with girls! The object-drawing exam was especially exciting because we sat in a circle, with the object to be drawn arranged in the middle, and opposite me was a 'vision of beauty', a girl from either the Portsmouth High School for Girls, or the Southern Grammar School. I sat staring at the 'vision' for ages, pretending to be looking at the object to be drawn. Suddenly I came to my senses and realised that there was only about a quarter of an hour to go before the work had to be handed in, and I had hardly made a mark on the paper. I remember the object to this day – it was a cylinder vacuum cleaner – but not the girl. With the sudden realisation that I had to do something PDQ, I started drawing at high speed without time to think; it was virtually eye-to-hand without intervention or interruption by the brain. When I looked at what I had drawn I was immediately aware that it was easily the best art that I had ever done. It was almost like a black-and-white photograph. I suppose that I was inspired: I never saw my inspiration again, but I achieved an excellent mark for object drawing. Despite this, when the results came out, once again there was disappointment. This time no distinctions – only three credits and four passes which still did not include English or English Literature. However, this time I was given a 'compensated pass' and awarded my School Certificate. I wondered why that could not have happened the first time when my results were better. In fact I was not to pass English at this level for another sixteen years.

Although I joined the Lower Sixth for the rest of the academic year, because I had effectively missed the first term, life was quite difficult and I was playing catch-up all the time and not making the progress to which I was accustomed. I decided to rethink my future, and instead of continuing with my Higher School Certificate studies I decided to apply to take the entrance exam to become an officer cadet at RAF Cranwell. Shortly after applying I realised that it would have been a good idea to have talk about it with Dad. When I told him what I had done, he said to me: '*Look son, if you take the exam I'm sure that you would pass without too much trouble, but once you got there you wouldn't' fit in. You don't come from the right background. Believe me, I've seen it and know how it works.*' As he had served in the RAF for more than ten years I listened to what he had said to me, took his advice and withdrew my application.

Nevertheless I knew that, because conscription was still in force, if I just left school I would be called up anyway, and directed to any of the Armed Forces at random and to any trade from cook to infantryman. So in order to choose the service and trade that appealed to me, I applied to become a Radio Fitter Apprentice in the RAF, and that was how I came to be at the point of 'going out into the big wide world'.

2

RAISING THE FLAG

Perhaps before I tell you about how I set out on that journey, I should go a little further back into my past. When I was born in 1931, Dad was in the Royal Air Force serving at RAF Cranwell. He was later posted to RAF Manston in Kent (my sister Pat was born in Kent in 1936) and then to RAF Lee-on-Solent. To begin with, we lived in Southways in Stubbington, but moved to Lee after Dad transferred in 1939 to the new Fleet Air Arm: the base became HMS Daedalus.

Our new home in Lee was at 24 Anglesea Road. As coincidence would have it, our new next-door neighbours, Mr and Mrs Cottrill and Brian their son, who was just six months older than me, turned out to be related to the Knowlton family – at Stubbington, in my last year at the school, I had shared a bench seat with Brenda Knowlton. Our desk was at the front on the right-hand side. I had enjoyed my time at the school, but maybe I had not always been as good as I pretended to be. I remember kissing Brenda in class when everyone was there (except the teacher). The Earth didn't move but I'd won the dare.

One of the first jobs that Dad did when we moved to Anglesea Road was to put up a post for the washing line. After duty one day he called in at a smallholding near Marks Road in Stubbington that sold, among other things, long poles for clothes-lines. He bought one that must been over fourteen feet in length, lashed it on to his bicycle and wheeled it along the road (on the airfield) to Anglesea Road, following the same path taken by Mum when she had, on one occasion, pushed Pat in her pushchair, with me in tow, from Stubbington to Lee. At home, Dad constructed an angle-iron triangular support which he set in a concrete base. Then the pole was raised, just as if we were explorers raising our flag on a newly discovered land. Instead of a flag, we had a clothes-line that was fixed to the house at the other end. Both ends could be raised or lowered by means of pulleys, which Dad had fitted. The clothes-line was fixed about two feet from the top and above this, at the top of the pole, Dad fixed a wire aerial so that we could receive programmes on our wireless. The aerial had ceramic insulators at each end and I thought they looked like white walnuts.

Within a few weeks of us moving to Lee-on-the-Solent, World War Two was declared. One of the popular comedians that we would listen to on the wireless at that time was Robb Wilton, who would start his droll monologues and sketches with the words *'The day war broke out.'*[1]

Well, on the day that war broke out it was sunny and warm. Jim Palmer, a lad of about my age who lived in Gosport Road, about a hundred yards away, ran out into the road and called out in an excited, cheerful voice: *'we're at war!'* As we were young and did not understand how serious it was, we were quite elated about it, thinking it would be a new exciting adventure. We were very soon to be disabused of that notion. The first effect was the introduction of rationing of bacon, butter and sugar, then up went the blackout curtains and the tape (similar to masking tape) that was put in criss-cross patterns across the windows, as if imitating the lattice windows of country cottages. The tape was intended to reduce the chance of people being injured by flying glass by keeping it in one piece, or at least large pieces, in the event of the windows being blown out by a bomb blast. Then we were issued with gas masks, which came in little cardboard boxes with a string attached as a shoulder strap.

Even with these changes in place, things remained much the same, and initially life carried on as normal. Lee-on-the-Solent was a village of two halves: those who lived on Marine Parade or in Manor Way and to west of it, who were the well-to-do and influential people. Those who lived at the eastern end, including Elmore, were neither

1 www.en.wikipedia.org/wiki/Robb Wilton

well-to-do nor influential. During the war there was some feeling of community, but not perhaps of shared hardship.

I started at Lee Junior School after the summer holidays. I enjoyed school, but it was a case of 'not getting too comfortable,' because, shortly after I had started there, the 'powers that be' decided to close the school and evacuate the children to safer places, away from the military establishments. Although many of the children in Lee-on-the-Solent were evacuated, Mum didn't want Pat or me to be sent away and so we stayed at home.

Although the war seemed to get off to a quiet start, it was not long before we were given a rude awakening, and a foretaste of what it was going to be like. It was during the first air-raid, though as no bombs were dropped in our immediate area, I suppose it didn't really count as an air-raid. It was at night and Dad was not at home because he was on duty in Daedalus. The rising and falling wailing pitch of the siren had alerted us to take cover. Mum grabbed Pat and me and we all went next-door and took shelter with the Cottrills in their hall. We all sat huddled on the floor and I stared at the rectangle of lino that covered the middle of the hallway and at the varnish on the remainder of the floor up to the skirting boards.

We could not hear any bombing taking place – all we could hear was the throbbing drone of squadrons of German bombers overhead, as they made their way to targets elsewhere in the country. This sound was accompanied by the irregular and intermittent sound of anti-aircraft gunfire. We had been sitting in the hall for a little while when someone said '*Hush – I think I can hear machine-gun fire.*' We all held our breath and listened, but the cause of the noise turned out to be my Mum. She was sitting with her knee resting against the panelling under the stairs, and because she was trembling so much it produced a rat-a-tat noise. We all laughed about it later … much later.

3
A CANNY TEACHER

As Lee school was closed, Mum enrolled Pat and me in a 'private school'. There were about a dozen others enrolled in this 'educational establishment', including my next-door neighbour Brian, at fees of 2/6 a week per pupil. In reality it was a large shed at the rear of the bungalow at 62 Raynes Road, and the whole enterprise was run by Mrs Good, assisted by her husband. She was a tall, angular, quite imposing lady with a beak nose. On reflection, she had a presence that reminded me a little of Queen Mary. Her husband was rather short and certainly not imposing. Inside the shed there was a large trestle table with wooden benches down the sides and along one end. Mrs Good would sit at the other end, at the top end of the table. On one wall there was a large poster showing all the ships of the Royal Navy in the 1937 Coronation Fleet review in the Solent.

I have very fond memories of this 'school' and still remember – over seventy years later – some of the things that we were taught there. We would chant out loud ... Northumberland, Newcastle on the Tyne, Durham, Durham on the Wear, Yorkshire, York on the Ouse ... and so on, to include all of the forty English counties and county towns and the rivers on which they stood. We also learnt our 'times tables' (eventually up to thirteen) by repeating them over and over again.

On a few occasions at break times we were taken to 'Cornerways', a house, which was run as a refined tea-rooms, on the corner of Queens Road, facing the Inn by the Sea on one side and Downing's Garage (now 'Fine Cars') on the opposite corner, where we each were given a real homemade lemonade and occasionally a cake.

I thought that Mrs Good was a first-rate teacher, bearing in mind that she had a group of children whose ages ranged from about four to fourteen. She would sometimes smoke when she was teaching, and as I have said, she had a rather large nose, and on quite a few occasions she would sit with a dewdrop hanging from the end of it, which was always a source of amusement to us pupils. It was a matter of speculation as to when, or if, the dewdrop would drop off.

One morning (records show that this was in July 1940) when we were having our lessons in the shed, we heard a succession of several explosions. We may have been a little startled, but as the siren had not sounded we didn't take too much notice. Eventually we discovered that the explosions were the sound of the Army or Navy blowing up sections of the ironwork of the pier at Lee Tower. Later we were able to see exactly what had been done. The pier had two ruddy great holes made in its ironwork structure. Or, as the papers reported it, the pier had been breached in two sections to prevent it being used by the Germans in the event of an invasion. A few years later when the Allies were preparing for D-Day, a temporary walkway was erected from the promenade to the jetty near the end of the pier: it took just a matter of hours.

In school, as well as learning our times tables by rote, we would, if the weather was fine, go outside for drawing lessons. My best-remembered outside lesson was when we went to the cliff tops opposite the end of Portsmouth Road and we had to draw 'Tower House', a hotel with a turret. It was on the west corner of Portsmouth Road and Marine Parade East.

On another day when we were at the school, the siren sounded, but we remained calm, and we all – more than a dozen of us – filed out and went across the waste ground at the end of Raynes Road to a Morrison brick air-raid shelter in a garden at the bottom of Seymour Road. I believe that the name of the family that lived there was Packer, and their son Eddy went to Mrs Good's school. We all sat in the shelter clutching our gasmasks in their little cardboard boxes. At some point we were told to put our gasmasks on and we discovered that by breathing out hard we could make the rubber side flaps vibrate and produce farting noises, which is exactly what we did.

The trouble with this game was that it made the visor mist up. Three or four of the older boys and girls were up to something else in the shelter – although it looked very interesting I never found exactly what they were doing, but there was a lot of giggling and guilty looks. The newspapers at the time noted March 1941: practice for an ARP simulated gas attack at Lee.

During the spring and summer of 1941, Mrs Good devised a competition to see who could grow (at home) the biggest crop from a single potato. We were each given a potato and told to cut it up so that each piece had an eye. I managed a row about nine feet long, and when the crop was harvested in September I won the competition with 22 pounds of potatoes. But Mrs Good was quite canny. She kept all of the potatoes that were taken in for weighing. For my prize I was awarded half a crown. With it I bought Mum a large bar of Cadbury's fruit and nut chocolate, and a packet of five Woodbines for Dad from Bennets's paper shop, which was in Portsmouth Road between Ryde Place and Wootton Road. Children at that time could buy cigarettes if they said the cigarettes were for their parents, and if the shopkeeper believed them. My honest face came to my aid. The cigarettes certainly weren't for me: in fact, I have never been tempted to smoke. I put this down to the fact that when I was young I saw a tramp in Gosport bend down and pick up, from a really dirty gutter, a discarded smouldering 'fag end', put it in his mouth and smoke what was left. This had a lifelong impact on me.

In the front room of the bungalow, hanging over the fireplace, was an ornate sword together with a photo of some relative of Mrs Good being presented with the sword by a member of the Spanish Royal Family. Mrs Good's bearing, attitude and speech created the impression that she was from a rather well-to-do family and the sword and picture tended to reinforce this impression. The front room was sometimes used as a classroom by Mr Good to teach spelling, but unfortunately it was usually in the afternoon and he'd occasionally had a pint or two over at the Inn by the Sea at lunchtime, so it was not unknown for him to nod off during the afternoon lessons. On one occasion, a small group of us were having a spelling session which consisted of Mr Good saying a word, and us writing down how we thought it was spelt. This lesson was of the snooze-foreshortened variety. Just after Mrs Good's shorter half had woken up with a start, we spent quite a few minutes unsuccessfully trying to contain our laughter when he asked us to spell the word 'piston'. We didn't get many words spelt that afternoon.

Less than a month after the breaching of Lee Pier, on Friday 16 August 1940 in the afternoon, there was a real air-raid. It was the middle of the school summer holiday; Pat and I were at home and fortunately we were playing not far from the house. When we heard the fear-inducing undulating wail of the siren, we quickly ran indoors. Mum grabbed us and took us to the Anderson air-raid shelter of a neighbour who lived just across the road in Brickland Terrace. Mrs P, in the spirit of the times, allowed any neighbours who did not have a shelter, to share hers. We all crammed in: Mrs P with her two young children, Mrs Cottrill, Brian, Mum, Pat and I plus two other women with a couple of very young children. It was a tight squeeze. It wasn't long before an aerial dogfight started above Elmore – it was very loud and sounded as if it was taking place directly above the shelter.

We soon discovered that there was a sailor in Mrs P's house (not her husband) who was 'staying over', and who had decided not to go down into the air-raid shelter when the siren sounded, because he preferred not to show his face to the inquisitive ladies of the neighbourhood. After the dogfight started Jolly Jack must have had a change of heart, and at the very last minute he decided to make dash for safety. The dogfight at that moment became rather intense and very noisy, and the women in the shelter pulled their children close in protective hugs. As the sailor dived into the shelter, he hit his back on the corrugated iron top of the doorway and fell onto the concrete floor. There was panic and shock when suddenly something – which turned out to be someone – was dumped into the shelter. The sailor was obviously in some pain and he thought that he had been hit by the gunfire.

I was too young at the time to appreciate the rest of the story, but it was explained to me later. Apparently, because he believed that he was dying, he made what he thought was a dying confession. It involved seeking forgiveness from his wife in Plymouth for the extramarital activities in which he had indulged with Mrs P in Brickland Terrace. This juicy bit of gossip became well repeated and worn around the edges, when accounts of the raid were exchanged during the following days.

This day of the dogfight was the day when 20 German Stuka dive-bombers attacked the airbase at Daedalus. They caused serious bomb damage, destroyed three hangers and 42 aircraft and killed 14 people including five civilians. Dad was on the base at Daedalus during this raid, and, although he would have been well aware of the devastation that had occurred, he never mentioned it: he knew what a worrier Mum was.

4

I MAKE A WISH

After the raid on Daedalus, the air-raids in the area became more frequent and Gosport began to suffer badly, so Dad decided to evacuate Mum, Pat and me to the home of Aunt Doris, Uncle Bill and Cousin Joan. They lived in Kilnhurst, near Sheffield. I expect that he realised that there would be more raids on Portsmouth and Gosport – and more there certainly were. We stayed at Kilnhurst until February 1941.

Dad was by trade a fitter rigger (or airframe mechanic) and he had a team that carried out maintenance and repair on the structure of aircraft. One can speculate that it was considered prudent to carry out this work out of the range of German bombers, following the devastation caused by the bombing raids on bases on the south coast. Whether this was the reason or not, Dad and his team were posted to Arbroath in Scotland where eventually he managed to get lodgings for Mum, Pat and me. So, at the end of February, we left Kilnhurst to follow him to Arbroath. We were to stay there for just a short time – a little over a month – and Pat and I went to the local school for about a week.

It is no exaggeration to say that I absolutely hated Arbroath. In the accommodation where we stayed, we had to share a combined bathroom and toilet with the family that lived there. The family were part of the local fishing community, and – well I don't know whether it was their diet or not, but I do know that whatever it was, a visit to the toilet after any of the family had used it was quite an ordeal. There is only so long that you can hold your breath. Mum and Dad didn't talk about this, but they were very surprised and concerned that the children of the house, who were about Pat's age, stayed up until the small hours of the morning, and as Pat had to share a room with the little girl of the family, she was not getting her proper sleep.

One late afternoon after school I walked the whole length of the promenade to a wishing well, threw in a coin and wished to go home. The next evening, Dad returned to the lodgings and said that he had been posted to Somerset and we were going home! ... so if you have aspirations to win the Lotto, then the wishing well in Arbroath might be worth considering.

On the long train journey home, although we were at war, there were still three classes of carriage. We, of course, travelled third class as we were 'NCO and other ranks with family'. The carriages were crowded, with the exception of first class, and Dad had difficulty in finding us space, but Dad – being Dad – did. There was what we later would consider to be an amusing incident on this tiring and dreary long journey, which was only bearable because we were going home. We stopped at Crewe, and Dad, always ready for a challenge, jumped off the train as it stopped and ran to the station buffet. He bought some mugs of tea and managed to get back on board, complete with the full mugs, hardly spilling a drop, as the train was just moving off. Mum was 'having kittens' – she was a worrier at the best of times, and these were not the best of times. As we travelled across London to Waterloo station there was an overpowering smell of smoke. Possibly the local population had become accustomed to it, because it didn't seem to bother them. We had breakfast in a makeshift café-cum-restaurant which I believe was run by the Women's Voluntary Service, just outside the station. The people all appeared to be tired and withdrawn, though many were helpful. On the platform as we were making our way to the Portsmouth train, Dad was carrying Pat's life-size baby doll, and he had it slung over his shoulder, with luggage in his other hand. A middle- aged woman came up to him and tapped him on the shoulder and said to him in a quite aggressive voice: '*that's not the way to carry a baby.*' She didn't even see the funny side of it when he showed her that it was only a doll.

5

BACK TO THE HOME FRONT

When we arrived at Portsmouth there were a lot of bombed buildings and in some cases whole streets had virtually disappeared. Possibly some of the debris had been removed, because it seemed as if there was just not enough debris for the houses that had once been there. All that was left were the holes that once had been the cellars, and a few small mounds of bricks here and there. I was told later that aerial land-mines had caused the horrendous damage. Apparently these mines were similar to normal sea-mines, but they were dropped by parachute and they exploded at the tops of the buildings, instead of lower down. I don't know for sure that it was aerial mines that caused all the devastation, but major devastation there most certainly was. On 10 January 1941, which was two months prior to our return, Portsmouth had suffered its worst raid, and many landmarks were wiped out or seriously damaged, including the Guildhall. Even the Pompey chimes were silenced.

We had missed some of the air-raids, but a few days after we returned, on 10 March 1941, more than a dozen people at a number of different addresses in Gosport were killed during a bombing raid. Despite this, Dad could not persuade Mum to go back to Kilnhurst, so we stayed in Lee-on-the-Solent.

It was during this spring, when Dad managed to get some leave, that he, together with the help of other men from the neighbourhood, dug a deep hole into which they built our Anderson shelter. It had a concrete floor with small interior concrete walls about two feet high, and when the arch-shaped pieces of corrugated iron had been bolted together, the whole structure was covered with about six inches of soil.

Later in the year, the Cottrills had a Morrison shelter built in their back garden. This type of shelter was an above-ground, strong, brick, windowless structure with a separate blast wall in front of the doorway. Before their shelter was built it was our turn to share our shelter with them. Sleeping in the shelters, even though there were bunks, was cold, miserable, damp and uncomfortable, and, as it was outside, it felt less secure than being indoors. '*What time did the all clear go?*' was the question everyone would ask the following morning, after a miserable night in the shelter. But because the sound of the 'All Clear' did not have the same impact as the alert siren, and possibly because we just too tired to be bothered, no-one seemed to know the answer to that question. It is quite surprising that even today the undulating sound of an alert siren evokes a sense of apprehension which is quite impossible to put into words. I am sure that all of those who lived through the war will know exactly what I mean, as will those who now live in war zones.

The raids continued for some while after we returned from Scotland, but life went on. In the morning after a raid, I would go out, like all of my contemporaries, to collect shrapnel. These irregular shards of metal, which were anything from an inch to six inches long, were mainly the remains of anti-aircraft shells, and although they were nice and shiny to start with, they very quickly became rusty.

After a while, nights in the shelter became something that we dreaded so much that we, like many of our neighbours, took to staying indoors. Mum, Pat and I used to sleep downstairs on a mattress under a kitchen table. It was at this time that I had developed a rather nasty abscess on my right shin, and it was so painful that I had been unable to sleep for quite a few nights. Mum had been told by the chemist that the best treatment for the abscess was to place a kaolin poultice on it. This involved making a sandwich of the kaolin (a kind of clay) between small pieces of linen and then heating it up by placing it in boiling water, and then putting it on the abscess whilst still warm. Mum did it all correctly except for the last part: she interpreted 'whilst still warm' as straight out of the boiling water and onto my leg. I expect that they heard my yell next door, but it did the trick and I enjoyed the first good night's sleep that I had had for many nights. In fact I slept right through that night's air-raid. Nevertheless, I still have the scar.

It is only in recent years that I have become aware of how much Mum's care for the welfare of me and Pat had been influenced by advertising. Looking at advertisements appearing in local newspapers of that time, constipation was responsible for just about everything that a young person could be prone to, from irritability to not doing well at school, lethargy, or in fact just about everything which nowadays we put down to being a teenager. So every Friday evening Pat and I were given a dose of Californian Syrup of Figs to cure our ills, both real and imaginary. Following this train of thought, it is worth mentioning that both during the war and after, toilet paper was not of the variety advertised today by cute little puppies. It was more akin to thin, shiny, greaseproof paper. And it was often not available at all: the main source of paper for use in the toilet, for most households, was newspaper torn into sheets which were then threaded into bundles on a piece of string and hung in the lavatory.

6

RUNNING WILD

Once our exile was over and we were home again, Pat and I returned to our 'private education'. At a council meeting at that time one of the councillors stated that there were 3,000 children of school age in Gosport and Lee who had not been evacuated or who had returned and *'were running wild and uneducated, because there are no schools open'*. That was not true for me – well in part it was not true – because I was enjoying the benefits of Mrs Good's teaching skills, and I was only running wild part-time. I suppose that, if I'm honest, I have to admit we did get up to quite a bit of mischief. On the seafront opposite Beach Road near to the promenade where the old railway line had once run, there was a derelict house which was boarded up to keep out people, for their own safety. Of course, to a group of us lads, this was a tempting invitation. We managed to 'find' some boards which, with a little persuasion, became loose, and on several occasions we went inside exploring. Usually we would scramble to the upper floor on a very rickety staircase, and peer out through the gaps in the boards that had been placed over the holes where there once had been windows. One day when we went into the ramshackle building we discovered that the whole staircase had completely collapsed. Fortunately for us, we had not been playing on the upper floor or on the staircase when it disintegrated. After this we tired of playing in the derelict house and turned our attention to some abandoned beach-huts near the remains of the old railway halt at Elmore. These huts became more and more derelict, possibly a result of us playing in them, and eventually they were removed.

A short stretch of road alongside Brickland Terrace, more or less a stubby extension of Anglesea Road, led to a track that went across the fields to Court Barn and then on to Cherque Farm. From the Elmore end of Lee-on-the-Solent this track was the main route for getting to Peel Common, and to the golf links. As youngsters we would go to the golf links, not to play golf but just to mess around and get up to mischief, playing in the bunkers and climbing some of the many silver birch trees that grew there and possibly (although not intentionally) damaging them.

This was a time of environmental unawareness and many of the activities in which we indulged, without much thought, would nowadays be seen as totally unacceptable. We would go 'bird nesting', which involved finding a bird's nest, and removing an egg: it would then have a pinprick hole made at each end, and the contents blown out. The objective of this activity was to build up a collection of as many different types of eggs as possible. One day when I was on one of these 'nature activities' with an older group of lads, one of the gang, the eldest son of the local newsagent, had climbed to the top of a tree and collected a pigeon's egg. He carefully made his way down with the egg safely in his mouth. When he got to the bottom branch of the tree, he hung there for a moment and then dropped the last three feet to the ground. Mistake! He never said what it tasted like but what came out of his mouth didn't look too appetising. We would also go foraging in the streams and ponds near the golf links, carrying nets and jam jars to collect sticklebacks and crested newts. Usually we would put them back where we had caught them, but occasionally we would take them home to show others – unfortunately not many of our finds survived that ordeal.

Court Barn, alongside the track across the field, was a good place to have fun. One day several of us were playing on the hay stored in the barn and the farmer caught us. As it was a 'fair cop', I politely and respectfully apologised and gave my real name and address. That evening a policeman called at our house and informed my parents that because I had been polite and apologised, the farmer would take no further action. Nevertheless it took several weeks before the shame of having a policeman call at the house wore off. Many years later, I became aware of how lucky I had been, when I read about what had happened to a couple of 14-year-old lads caught by the same farmer later that year. They ended up in front of the Beak (as the Magistrate was known). They had taken some hay from a field (for their rabbits) and the owner, Colonel House, had caught them and they had been charged with theft. Colonel House said that he had brought the action against them because he had suffered so much damage to hay and straw ricks and fodder. The case was considered proved but was dismissed, with the two boys paying costs of seven shillings and sixpence each.

The episode at Court Barn was not my only run-in with the constabulary during this what I have sometimes referred to as the rebellious phase of my life. I was with Ronnie from Raynes Road and we were playing in an empty, bomb-damaged, derelict shop in Marine Parade opposite Lee Tower. The windows had all been blown out as well as the door, and the inside of the shop was completely empty except for an old orange box. On one wall there was a block of brown Bakelite light-switches, some of which had not been damaged. For some reason which I have never been able to fathom, we decided to remove them. We didn't see it as stealing or worse, the looting which it really was. We hadn't planned this 'light-switch removal', although you may find that hard to believe when I tell you that – unbeknown to Dad – I had one of his screwdrivers with me.

We had removed the three or four undamaged ones when I happened to look out through the hole where the windows should have been. I saw a policeman pull up over the road on his bicycle; it was still daylight and this must have been part of his regular beat. After he had parked his bike alongside a telephone booth, he looked over in our direction and strolled over, almost with a John Wayne swagger. Before he reached the shop we quickly threw the switches, together with the screwdriver, into the storage space under the window. When he came in, he asked for our names and addresses. After we told him, he asked us what we were doing in the remains of the shop. '*We're just messing about sir,*' we replied. '*Well you're not supposed to be in here*,' he said. '*Off you go*.' We didn't need twice bidding; we left pretty promptly, headed east (towards Elmore), did a left turn, ran round the corner into Pier Street, then after a few yards turned left through the entrance to the flats which also led to waste ground behind the buildings. We ran diagonally across this waste ground and then through another of the flats' entrance passageways, so that we were now back in Marine Parade facing the Tower, but we were to the west of the shop where we had been caught, and the policeman had seen us leave briskly going east. Peering out, we saw the policeman come out of the bomb-damaged shop, get on his bike and quickly cycle off in the direction that we had taken. No sooner was he out of sight than we were back at the scene of the crime. I was hoping to reclaim Dad's screwdriver, but there was no sign of it. We saw the switches had been retrieved and placed on the 'orange box', so we gathered them up, nipped over the road to the beach and committed them to a watery grave. Then slowly, very slowly and nervously, we made our way home.

The policeman had been and gone before I arrived home and Dad was not best pleased; he had been shown the screwdriver by the policeman but he had not identified it, because it had a broad arrow stamped on it. Apparently the policeman had returned to the derelict shop and had discovered that all of the 'evidence of the crime' had disappeared, so no further action was to be taken, and of course he kept the screwdriver. '*You are not to play with that Ronnie again!*' Dad said, and no doubt Ronnie was told never to play with me again. But we did.

Rebel

The policeman knew Anglesea Road quite well. He occasionally visited a house in the road where the man who managed the NAAFI in Daedalus lived. Of course, during the war we were limited in the amount of food that we could have because of the rationing, and there were certain rumours and murmurings about these visits, and mutterings about 'black market'. I did wonder if Dad had hinted about this to the policeman, who was not known for his leniency, because from then on, the policeman was not seen making any more visits to the NAAFI manager's home. Perhaps they rescheduled their rendezvous location, or maybe the purpose of their alleged meetings was just gossip.

During the winter following our return from Scotland, Dad was taken to hospital to have an emergency operation which was needed to make good an appendicitis operation that had been performed over two years earlier at Haslar Hospital. On this occasion he was taken to Park Prewett Hospital near Basingstoke. Before the war it had been a mental hospital, but it had been seconded, in part, for use as a surgical hospital during the war.

Visiting Dad was very difficult, but Mum took Pat and me on at least three occasions. It meant very early starts. Because it was winter we left in the dark and came home in the dark. The journey from home to the hospital took nearly three hours. We had to walk from our house to the bus stop and catch a bus to Fareham bus station, then a walk of nearly a mile to the railway station, a train ride to Basingstoke, and finally a bus ride of about a mile, which seemed much further because the bus was very old and slow and it struggled to get up hills. It really did seem to take forever to get there. It was during the coldest part of the winter of a year that was particularly cold. On one of these treks, early in the morning, we were huddled on the station at Fareham trying to keep out of the bitterly icy northerly wind that was blowing down the platform. We had been there a little while, getting colder and colder, when a serviceman (I think he was an army corporal) came on to the platform. When he saw Mum's plight with two children in tow he went straight to the ticket office and demanded quite forcefully that they opened the waiting room, which had been closed and locked up till then. Although there was no fire in the waiting room, it was a great relief to get out of that wind.

To compound Dad's problem, while he was in the hospital some complication resulted in him having to undergo a throat operation, within days of the initial surgery. It so happened that this operation took place on a day that we were visiting him and we saw him not long after he came out of the operating theatre. He looked dreadful and I thought he was going to die. We were sitting round his bed staring at him, probably as white-faced as he was, when what must have been the Matron came into the ward: '*What on Earth are these children doing here?*' she demanded of the ward nurse '*Get them out of here!*' That turned out to be a very short visit for a very long journey.

On our next visit it was such a relief to see him looking much better and sitting up in bed. While he was recuperating, for his occupational therapy he learnt how to make soft toys, and because he was well-skilled in sewing, he produced some excellent sewn items. Dad had learnt how to sew as a young man working on trawlers, when he had to repair the nets. One of the proud claims of Mum was that, when I was born, Dad had knitted most of my baby clothes. It was virtually unheard of for a man to do anything like that in those days. When we left that day Pat had a colourful toy elephant, and I had a hand-sewn leather wallet. Within a month, Dad was back on duty at Daedalus.

7

BETWEEN THE 'B' AND THE 'ANG'

Eventually so many youngsters returned from being evacuated that Lee Junior School found a location and re-opened. The new location was required because the school buildings had been taken over for some other purposes. For a while lessons were held in the rooms above the Lee Library for the senior classes and, for the younger pupils, in what was called 'The Bungalow' on Portsmouth Road. It was on the same side as 'Cornerways' but nearer to the seafront. It was there that Pat went to classes. She said that there were brick walls in front of the windows to prevent them from being blown in by bomb blast.

Although I had enjoyed my time at Mrs Good's school, it was good to be back at Lee Junior School, especially when we moved back to the proper premises. It was just after the school returned to its normal site that I first met Ronnie and we started getting into mischief. Also it was about this time, in the summer of 1941, that free school milk started to be given out at school. We used to get a small bottle of milk – one third of a pint. One of the duties I had for a while was that of 'milk monitor' which involved giving out a bottle of milk and a straw to each pupil, and when everyone had finished, collecting up the empties and putting them back in the crate.

Another role which I filled for a short while was that of 'ink monitor', and filled is a most apposite word because my role was to fill the inkwells from a large bottle of ink. The filling task was carried out on an ink-stained wooden tray on a bench at the front of the classroom. I then had to carry the tray of filled inkwells to each desk in turn, slotting an inkwell into the hole that was made for this purpose. The lifting of the large bottle of ink was a surprisingly difficult task for youngsters with small hands, like mine. You could always pick out the ink monitor; it would be the one with the most heavily ink-stained hands. The ink was as malevolent as ever. I remembered it from my days at Stubbington School. It was an evil liquid, which had the capability of jumping off your pen, on to your exercise book. It could even sneak unseen on to your fingers and then spread itself just about everywhere. The pens were of the same style that we had used in Stubbington, with round wooden shafts, which had the uncanny knack of being able to attract the ink. The nib was slotted into a metal fixing at the end of the shaft. To say that this was always a messy lesson is rather like saying Mount Everest is quite a large hill.

There was one occasion when a policeman came into the classroom to talk to us. When he addressed the class, he said that the police were aware of the fact that some of the boys in the school had been 'acquiring', and had in their possession, ammunition. He then added that if we handed in any ammunition, then no further action would be taken. Of course, as he was a policeman we all believed that if he told us to, we would all have to empty our pockets and turn them inside out. There was a prompt line of boys making their way to the front of the class. In one class alone, on that one day, there were over a hundred rounds of live rifle ammunition, in the form of 303 bullets, handed in. I didn't have any, and I turned out my pockets to prove it. The reason I didn't have any was because my stash was at home, hidden in a suitcase under my bed. My hoard even included a couple of cannon shells which I had acquired by a bit of 'astute' trading. These cannon shells were about six inches long. That evening after dark I went to the beach and threw the lot over the barbed wire into the sea at Elmore.

At school there was one activity that I particularly enjoyed and it was the mental arithmetic sessions of twenty questions. It was how Mr Nixon, the headmaster, would start each day. I was proud of my mental arithmetic, and hated to get anything less than twenty out of twenty correct. To this day there is a standing joke in our family regarding a question that occurred during one session.

'If it takes three minutes to boil one egg, how long does it take to boil four eggs?' ... my contention was that it must be 12 minutes. Mr Nixon said the answer was three minutes. I put up my hand up and was told to stand up. I said that the lesson was supposed to be mental arithmetic, and not cookery. '*What if it was only a small saucepan?*' This was sternly dismissed. I sailed pretty close to the wind that day and was told in no uncertain terms to '*Sit down.*'

On the subject of eggs, some of Dad's resourcefulness must have rubbed off on Mum because in 1942 we were the first family in our area to use the new dried powdered eggs, which became available to supplement our egg ration. Quite a few families were very wary of 'dried eggs' and in some cases it was many months before they even tried them.

At school on another occasion, sometime later, Mr Nixon brought a grass snake into the school and passed it round the class so that everyone could feel that it was not slimy, and was in fact quite pleasant to handle. Most of the girls and even some of the boys were none too keen to handle the snake, but I was quite keen to give it a try: it was soothing and I enjoyed holding it.

I suppose it was the Jekyll and Hyde nature of my character that between the age of ten and twelve, in the winter months I was very much a loner, but in the summer months I wanted to be part of a group or gang and to 'hang out' on the beach or 'up the Tower' or to go scavenging over the Ranges or on the beach. To join the gang that eventually I was allowed to 'tag along with', both Brian and I – who were initiated at the same time – had to demonstrate our suitability to be members by doing a running jump off the cliffs near the red-flag hut at Elmore. It was a drop of over twelve feet on to a sloping shingle beach. That part of the beach was known as the 'Rocks', but actually there were no rocks, just a collection of large concrete blocks. The largest were about 30 feet long and 6 feet wide and deep arranged in an irregular heap. The tides and shifting shingle over time had shuffled them into a disarrayed but interesting jumble, which appeared to be slightly changed by every tide. Brian and I passed the test without any breakages and were accepted as 'affiliated members'.

Sometimes when I think about it, I am quite surprised that so many of us managed to eventually become pensioners, not so much because of enemy activity, but because of the sheer stupidity of what we did. When I think of all the stupid things that I have done in my life (and by the time you get to my age you have done quite a few), I would say that number one must be standing on what we believed to be an unexploded bomb. It was rusty, about four feet long and about a foot in diameter with fins and it was lying on its side just above the high-water mark on the beach towards the Stokes Bay end of the Ranges. Several of us stood on it in turn as an act of bravado or a dare. I think that we had the childish belief that we could jump clear between the B and ANG of the explosion if it went off. Not long after this, there was a rumour in circulation which made us think about what we had done. According to the rumour, a sailor was killed when he disturbed an unexploded bomb and it went off. It was alleged to have happened on the beach opposite 'Skippers Garage' on Marine Parade East, not far from where the old derelict building had once stood.

Although we had got away with our game with what we thought was an unexploded bomb, there was an occasion the following year when things did go with a bang. Over the Warren there was an area where the military practised hand-grenade throwing. Obviously we were not supposed to go there, but of course we did (when it was not being used). There were quite a few trenches that didn't seem to have any purpose. A couple of them were about six feet deep, three feet wide and about twenty-five feet long. Brian and I managed to lower ourselves into one of these deep ones, then discovered that it was not so easy to get out, and we were only able to do it with great difficulty. Eventually we succeeded by grabbing on to the roots of nearby gorse bushes which were growing out of the side of the trench. There were other trenches in the area that were only about four feet deep with longer runs, so we stuck to playing our war games in them after that. During one of our games we found what Brian said was a hand-grenade fuse. He had recently joined the Army cadets, and was pretty certain what it was, so we took 'our find' home. We were messing about with it in his back garden when Brian suddenly yelled *'Run!'* I jumped over the wire fence between our gardens but didn't quite make our back door; Brian scooted indoors and slammed their back door, and then there was an almighty bang. The exploding fuse made a half-inch deep crater in the concrete about six feet from their back door. This small crater was to be a reminder of our 'near miss' for quite a few years after that. At the time we were suitably chastised by our mothers. Needless to say, it didn't stop us from continuing our quest to find more 'items of interest'.

Despite the earlier school visit by the constabulary, many young lads, including me, resumed 'acquiring of ordnance' by scavenging on the firing ranges in the evening, after the soldiers had finished for the day. Mostly we would get on to the Ranges from the beach. At that time the cliffs extended further towards the sea and near to where the angling club clubhouse is now situated was the red-flag hut. In this hut there would be someone on duty whose responsibilities included hauling up a red flag when firing was in progress to let everyone that they must 'KEEP OUT', and also to make sure that no-one went past the red flag.

If the firing had apparently ceased and the flag was still up, it was customary for youngsters, myself included, to sneak along the beach close to the cliffs and then try to clamber around the end of the perimeter wire fence that extended down to the low tide water's edge. Alternatively we would follow the fence inland and crawl under the wire in places where small gullies had been dug out by wild animals. As the gorse-covered bank that sloped down to the rifle range on the other side of the wire was a giant rabbit warren, it was most likely rabbits that had dug the holes, and which we had enlarged. These 'entrances' were much more difficult to get to unobserved when anyone was on duty at the hut.

On our scavenging expeditions to the Ranges it would be most unusual not to find at least a couple of live rounds on each visit. Nevertheless, even with our most diligent scavenging, we never found all of the lost bullets, as a later occurrence would show.

Not only were the Ranges a source of illicit 'finds', they were also a great adventure playground where, instead of slides and see-saws, there were the target-raising mechanisms in front of the butts, the turntables on the narrow gauge railway and sometimes even a railway trolley. Also the area was frequented by sailors and their girlfriends, and on a number of occasions we came across couples engaged in alfresco amorous activities. When the older lads in the group explained to the rest of us, in very descriptive (coarse) language, what was going on, I became appraised of the details that would be missing from the talk which Dad gave me, several years later, when I was about to venture out into the 'big wide world'.

Gorse fires over the Warren and Browndown ranges were a regular occurrence and it was recorded in the press in September 1946 that during one of these gorse blazes 'bullets lost during training operations went off a frequent intervals but no-one was injured.' I witnessed this fire at close range and the most awful thing about it was watching how the fire was spread. At the bottom of the gorse-covered embankment was the narrow-gauge rail track, and it was expected that it would provide a fire break. But many rabbits, with their fur in flames and fleeing the fire, jumped across the track and set fire to the gorse and grass on the other side.

8

THE LOST GOLDMINE OF LEE

The more we learnt about our neighbours after we moved into Anglesea Road, the more we realised that there were extended families all living in close proximity to one another. At the Gosport Road end of Brickland Terrace there was Granny Sherwood and in the bungalow effectively next-door in Gosport Road, just 25 yards away, was her son with his wife and two daughters. At the other end of the Terrace lived Mr and Mrs Goodwin; her brother 'Young Mr Horne' lived opposite, with his wife and son, in the first bungalow in Wootton Road, which backed onto our house. Next to the Terrace was a pig farm, complete with barn, that belonged to the father of 'Young Mr Horne', and of course he was known as 'Old Mr Horne'. Fortunately for us we lived up-wind from the pig farm. That is, when the wind came from the normal prevailing quarter – the south west. On the rare occasions when the wind blew from the north east in the summer, it tended to pong a little.

Old Mr Horne was often to be seen with his horse and cart as he went to and fro between his farm and HMS Daedalus to collect swill for the pigs. One day he passed a bunch of us lads as he was on his cart on the way back from the kitchen on the base, complete with a cartload of old drums filled with swill. He called out: '*do you like ship's chocolate?*' The answer obviously was yes, at which he threw down to us several unwrapped bars. To this day I am not quite sure what 'ship's chocolate' was – it certainly wasn't Cadbury's. Anyhow we thanked him, wiped off any excess pieces of extraneous material, ate the 'chocolate' and more or less enjoyed it. In those days we didn't wash our hands quite so frequently. This is probably how we built up our immunity against many illnesses ... and of course in other cases how we caught them.

Behind the pig farm there were fields that stretched to the Warren, which later became known as the Wild Grounds. Following on round from the pig farm, along Wootton Road, on the field side, there was a smallholding where it was possible to buy vegetables. This was at a time when the population were urged to 'make do and mend' and to 'dig for victory'. To this end, the Council ordered that part of the Recreation Ground should be ploughed up so that the land could be used for the growing of vegetables. Further along Wootton Road where it curves, on the field side and about 20 yards from the road, there was a large hole about 50 yards in diameter and about 30 feet deep. It had a great deal of rubbish in it, and at one time it may have been as a rubbish tip as it was known at the 'Dump'.

We used it as a play area: this also, in all probability, resulted in more building up of our immunities to goodness knows what diseases. Digging caves into the sandy sides of the 'Dump' and attempting to chop down trees on its rim were two popular activities. The choice of activity usually depended upon whether we had seen a film about lumberjacks or gold miners. On the opposite side of the road was a plot of land where Miss Walsh, who lived in a large house at the Anglesea Road end of Seymour Road, kept chickens. Miss Walsh also owned a large piece of land that ran from her house up to Anglesea Road. My sister Pat remembers being chased from it by Miss Walsh, who was wielding a pitch-fork.

The Seymour Road rectangular plot was bounded on two sides by 'ten foot ways' and by Seymour Road and Anglesea Road on the other two sides. Most of it was overgrown with a plantation of brambles. There were a few trees in one corner, near to Miss Walsh's house, and a row of trees where it was bounded by Anglesea Road. A group of us, fresh from our exploits of digging into the side of the dump, decided to dig a vertical mine shaft among the trees near Miss Walsh's house. We ended up digging a hole about four feet in diameter and seven feet deep. I should point out that at both sites of our mining activities, the soil was very sandy and the digging was relatively easy, but with hindsight, was also seriously dangerous. A few days after we had completed our digging we discovered that the 'lost gold mine of Lee' had disappeared. Pat told me that Miss Walsh had found out what we were up to and 'approached' one of the parents, who had then filled in the hole.

The row of about half-a-dozen trees which bordered Anglesea Road was about twenty feet high and faced three of the houses a few doors down from us. It was a very popular play area for us youngsters, particularly after any Tarzan film, but not so popular with two lady spinsters who lived opposite the trees. One day when we climbing through the trees, I reached the end of the short row and was demonstrating my prowess in getting down from a fairly high branch without climbing down. Of course I was showing off as usual. I had worked out that the further that I went out on the branch, the more it would bend and I would have less distance to drop. Not a good move! The branch broke and, as I was swinging at the time, I landed on my back. I was so winded that I was unable to speak, so someone ran to get my mum. When she arrived at the scene, she leaned over me and said in a worried but consoling voice: '*speak to me Johnny, speak to me.*' Eventually I managed to speak .... I wished I hadn't – she gave me a quite a hard smack for frightening her.

We had a game which we played when it had rained and filled the roads with puddles. Using sticks, we would scrape 'channels' between the puddles, joining them up, and then we would scrape a channel to the edge, and off the road in places where the land was lower than the road – thus we constructed our own 'lakes' and 'swamps' by the roadside.

There was a great deal more open space in those days. There were houses only on the east side of Anglesea road. That is, they backed onto Wootton Road. Also there were only a few bungalows on the north side of Gosport Road. Facing our house was what we called a 'Green', but in actual fact was just an overgrown uneven area of bushes and ditches: it was a first-rate play area. Looking from our upstairs front windows across the 'Green', the nearest house was in Cross Road, which was over two hundred yards away. To the left we could see the backs of the houses in Seymour Road.

Apart from the lady who shared, among other things, her air-raid shelter, a couple of her neighbours in Brickland Terrace are etched in my memory. The terrace faced the side of our back garden so we were able to observe some of the things that went on in the terrace. At that time the Brickland properties had only outside toilets, and in the second house starting from the Gosport Road end, the 'lady of the house' was in the habit of emptying the chamber pot straight out of the front upstairs bedroom window. Dad pointed out to her in a rather forthright manner, as was his way, how unhygienic this was. He always called a spade a spade.

Next in the terrace, the third one along, lived a Mr and Mrs Gibbs. They were well past middle age and she was a devout Catholic who attended church with a clinical regularity. Unfortunately Mr Gibbs had a mental problem, and he was frequently to be seen standing at the upstairs window during air-raids shouting out: *'calling all German air bombers to bomb England'*. He was a very sad case and no danger to anyone. His wife dedicated her life to caring for him.

Returning to the story of the sailor and the air-raid shelter, I realise now that people were no more or no less moral than they are today and it would be unfair to be too critical of the behaviour of people at that time. It was a very uncertain period and many didn't know if they or their spouse would be still alive the next day. After what, in some cases, was a matter of years of separation, many of the wives left behind would be in need of human companionship both emotional and biological, with all that involved. So I hope you will not think it too unkindly of me, in looking back and seeing the humorous aspects of some of the hanky-panky that went on, which of course as a child I didn't understand.

It was a couple of years before I became acquainted with the theory, and a decade after that before I fully passed the practical test. I remembering hearing the barber ask customers in a quiet voice if they would like 'something for the weekend'. At the time I thought they were buying some sort of shampoo. That is, before I went on those educational trips to the Ranges, where some of those items, which had been used and discarded, were pointed out and explained to me. Condoms were known then as 'French letters' or 'Johnnies' and were only sold in chemists from under the counter or in barber shops. It would be a very brave unmarried young man who would chance going into a chemist's to ask for a pack of 'Durex'. In any case, it is most likely that he would have been refused.

There were unconfirmed stories about young men going through the shop door with such a purchase in mind, but when confronted by a female assistant, left with cough lozenges instead. It is hardly surprising that a number of my contemporaries a few years later 'had to get married', as the saying goes. In other instances there were secrets (which really weren't secret within families) which involved additions to the family. Also there were occasions when some young men had to go before the 'Beak' for jumping the gun on the law regarding girls being sixteen years old. 'Having carnal knowledge' was the language used in those court cases, and getting the under-age girl pregnant, had sometimes been the result.

After the 'friendly shelter lady' and her family moved out, not very long after the shelter episode, Mrs Wort moved into the house. Everyone knew her as 'Dubby' and I believe that she was related in some way to Mrs Cottrill. Her husband was serving in the army, and she had two young daughters – Freesia and Cynthia. Tragically Dubby's husband – after having survived all the fighting – was killed in Europe shortly after the hostilities had finished. Apparently he died as a result of an accident when he was directing military vehicles.

9

A BUNCH OF 'RATTYS'

Throughout the war years, in the summer, my life – like that of many of my contemporaries – revolved around the beach, when we were able to get on to it. As a general rule, if the tide was in we would be 'out', on the beach. Many of us who had been influenced by the Tarzan films would often not wear shoes and became quite hardened to running barefoot on the shingle beach, and on the way there and back, adept at avoiding where dogs had done their business on the pavement. There were few canine restrictions then, other than the fact that all dog owners were required to have a licence for every dog that they owned. Dogs were supposed to be kept under control, but it was quite common to see dogs chasing the occasional car or one of the many cyclists. It was quite unusual to see a dog being taken for a walk on a lead.

Apart from the Ranges, the Warren was also a great adventure playground, as illustrated by the hand-grenade fuse incident. On the Warren was an area known as 'Hangman's Hollow' not far from Apple Dumpling bridge, where it was alleged that a man had hanged himself and that his ghost haunted the area. I don't know it this was just a story that was circulated to try to frighten off youngsters like us. If that was the plan, it failed miserably. Rather than being put off, the place became clothed in a more interesting mantle. Not far from 'Hangman's Hollow' was a track which is now part of Sandhill Lane, and there was a 'NO TRESPASSERS' notice nailed to one of the trees alongside the track. No doubt you can guess what the three of us did. We were cautiously walking (or, to be more honest, quietly sneaking) along the track when we came to a cottage down in a dip. It looked very creepy. Of course it is now long gone, but it was near where the Alver Valley boardwalk is now situated. Well, we were just about level with the cottage when we realised that we had been spotted by what in all probability was the gamekeeper. He had a gun and was on his bike. I don't think ghosts ride bikes and have guns. He chased us down the track. We ran hell-for-leather into the Warren and then dived over a bank and lay flat in a cornfield for about half an hour before venturing out. We didn't chance our arm by going down that track again.

The river Alver more or less formed the eastern boundary of the Warren, which we considered to be our 'territory'. It happened that one day one of the gang came into possession of a tin bath about five feet long – either his mother had no further use for it or she didn't know that he had taken it. Between us we carried it all the way to the Warren, and when we got to the river, each of us in turn stretched out in the bath and – with our arms over the side – paddled over and back across the river at a point where it was about ten feet wide. That adventure over, we carried the bath back to Elmore. The next day we reconvened and took the bath down to the beach and tried it in the sea. I was the first to have a go and fortunately I was wearing my bathers because, when I got into the bath, it promptly rolled over and sank, possibly because of the increased buoyancy in salt water. Whatever the reason we were ruddy lucky, because if it had turned turtle on the river Alver, one of us would have been dumped into smelly muddy water and would have had to clamber out over the smelly muddy banks and would have ended up looking like a smelly muddy 'creature from the Black Lagoon'.

It was later that same summer when we indulged in what, with hindsight, was a more foolhardy and dangerous water-based escapade. It took place in the sea at Elmore, near to where the bath hadn't floated our boat, and it occurred shortly after we had seen a sunken treasure film. Four of us were in a dingy (I've no idea how we came by it) ready to re-enact what we had seen at the cinema. One of the gang, Denis, who lived in Seymour Road, was 'chosen' to be the diver. We tied a belt around his waist, to which we had attached some large stones. Then, with a rope tied round his waist and a long piece of garden hose held to his mouth, he jumped into the water. I am not absolutely sure whether he was a willing volunteer or not, and I think that it is reasonable to assume that it may have been an assisted entry into the water. The boat was in about ten feet of water at the time. After a couple of minutes we became a bit concerned because nothing seemed to be happening, so – with some difficulty – we hauled him back into the dingy. He was coughing and spluttering and obviously had not been able to breathe through the hosepipe several feet down. I have jokingly referred to his staring eyes after this, but it must have been quite scary for him.

It was also about this time when there were several of us in a 'borrowed' rowing boat on a moat that was a 'tributary' of the river Alver. We were near where the river went under the military road which is now Browndown Road. The moat ran parallel to and on the sea side of Browndown Road from the Alver River towards Lee-on-the-Solent for a couple of hundred yards, almost to the Small Arms School gates. It has long since been filled in and overgrown. On the opposite side of the road, the level of the land was much lower and was a swampy marsh which was later filled in and became the Kingfisher caravan park. At that time the road, which belonged to the military, was closed one day each year to ensure that it remained under their control. There were no pavements and although the road had been covered with tarmac at some time in its distant past, it was in a very poor state of repair with numerous potholes which resulted in a number of accidents. This military road, which was the main road from Gosport to Lee-on-the-Solent, ran on the sea side of the main building of the Small Arms School and even to this day, nearer to Lee, remnants of it can still be seen on the other side of the wire fence alongside the Lee end of Privett Road.

There we were, a bunch of 'Rattys' from 'Wind in the Willows', just messing about in a boat. A soldier walking along the road and heading back from Gosport to the Small Arms School called out to us: '*Hey lads how about a lift?*' The leader of the gang called back '*OK*' and we rowed to the bank of the moat. The soldier clambered aboard, nearly capsizing us in the process, and we rowed him the couple of hundred yards or so to the end of the moat near the Small Arms School. He could have walked the distance in half the time it took us to row it, but it was just a bit of fun. As he left, he complimented us on our rowing, but in reality, we weren't all that good.

Considering the fact that most of us learnt to swim by being thrown into the sea, it was surprising that, to the best of my knowledge, there were no drowning incidents among my peers when I was growing up, although it was a close call for at least one or two of some of those that I was with in the summer of 1945. A gathering of a couple of dozen of us boys and girls were having a day on the beach near the present-day sailing club, when some American sailors in an engine-powered whaler pulled onto the beach near us. Their ship must have been one of a small fleet that was anchored out in the Solent. One of them called out and asked if anyone fancied a trip in the boat and about six of us said that we would. Although there were almost a dozen girls in the collection of youngsters on the beach, none of them opted to go in the whaler. We realised later that the presence of the girls was the most likely reason why the Americans had invited us for a trip, and we recalled a popular joke of the time which said that when the American servicemen came back after the war they didn't recognise the place – because all of their girlfriends had left school. I'm sure it's not true ... well not entirely sure because there were rumours. However, when we were about a quarter of a mile out to sea, the sailors said that they had to get back to their ship and told us to jump off. It was a very close call for two of the group, who could only just swim, but we all made it back to the beach safely.

10

A VILLAGE OF TWO HALVES

For Mum, as for many housewives at that time, the only way to keep food cool was by placing it near the fine wire mesh that formed the small window on the outside wall of the pantry. Therefore shopping was more or less a daily chore for most housewives, who would do their shopping mainly in the High Street. Generally it would be very busy with people queuing to be served at the butcher's, fish shops, grocer's and greengrocer's. Shopping took a lot of time. Only one or two people would be served at time, and the serving process was very slow and laborious. In most of the shops the goods would be displayed behind the counter (also some would be kept out of sight under it), and it was never a case of the purchaser choosing their own food items. The person serving would ask the customer what they wanted, how much or how many, then, if and when necessary, ask the customer to pass over their ration book to make sure that they had enough coupons. The proprietor or assistant would tear out the appropriate number of coupons or cancel them, more often than not with an indelible pencil, select the items, do the weighing, if necessary work out the cost, take the money and ring it up on the till, hand the customer their change if there was any, wrap the purchase (often in newspaper) and hand it over. If more than one item was purchased, the person behind the counter would work out the cost, sometimes on a piece of paper, which meant that the customer was always at the mercy of the arithmetic of the shop assistant. The whole process was extremely time-consuming, which was the main reason why so many queues were very long.

It was very important for shoppers not to forget early-closing day, because shops, as required by law, would close at 12.30pm or 1pm. If a shop failed to close on the specified day the owner or manager would be taken to court and fined, and they would also risk their licence to trade being withdrawn.

Early-closing day rules continued into the 1950s. In December 1952 the proprietor of 'Valentines', one of the shops in the Parade opposite Lee Tower, was fined £1 for 'failing to close their shop on early closing day'. In Lee-on-the-Solent early closing day was Thursday, so if anything was forgotten on that day it was a case of going without, or taking a bus ride to Gosport or Fareham where early closing was on Wednesday.

During the war it was the general belief of the residents who lived in the east end of the village, that all of the better-quality groceries and cuts of meat were put on one side (under the counter) for the better-off residents who lived at the west end of the village, and this unequal treatment gave rise to a certain amount of resentment. *'As if they didn't have it cushy enough already'* was the often-heard complaint. The discontent about the preferential treatment was not just idle speculation and suspicion based on jealousy, but based on the observations of those 'Eastenders' who were in the employ of the 'Westenders', and the shop assistants who worked in the High Street. Despite the country being at war, Lee-on-the-Solent was still a village of two halves.

Deference reigned supreme. Many of those favoured in the shops were officers' wives, who formed the main clientele of the upmarket Hove-to tea-rooms which was the first establishment in the High Street on the left as you entered it from the west or Milvil Road end.

In a conversation that a group of us youngsters 'accidently' overheard (well, you know what kids are like) which happened as we passed a conspiratorial gaggle of housewives standing in a queue outside one of the shops in Elmore, the topic of the gossip was one of the 'toffee-nosed' officers' wives. 'S*he's no cause to be so hoity-toity .... all fur coat and no drawers.*' Us youngsters all assumed that they were referring to the subject of the gossip going out inappropriately dressed, and thinking that the expression must be an upmarket version of 'red hat no knickers'. We all thought it was very amusing. It was much later that I discovered that both the expressions referred to behaviour and not attire, and that a red hat was almost part of the uniform worn by the women that Dad would eventually warn me about.

Apart from the provisions purchased in the High Street and a few local shops, there were other things, such as bread and milk, which were delivered by the same delivery vans that had called at the house when we lived in Stubbington: Sandy's the baker, Williams from Titchfield and Tom Parker's milkmen from Cams Alders. Williams only came round once a week, but milk was delivered every day (except Sunday), and bread was delivered every few days. Milk was delivered to just about every house, but not all families had the bread delivered because some of them preferred to buy their bread in the High Street or at the baker's in Elmore.

Among the small collection of shops in Elmore opposite the Inn by the Sea was a Post Office, which had one of those cylindrical red postboxes standing outside. During the war it had its top painted a pale green, and we were told that this paint would change colour in the event of a gas attack, in which case we had to put on our gasmasks. I think it's almost certain that by the time anyone noticed the change of colour on the top of the postbox, provided that you were tall enough to see it – which I most certainly wasn't – everyone in the area would already be dead.

In those days a Postmaster was a highly respected person and widely accepted as a character referee. On at least two occasions I went to see Mr Aguter, the Postmaster, to sign forms to attest to my good character, which he did. How little he knew!

IIII

THE ODD BOMB OR TWO

As the war had progressed we had all become a bit blasé about air-raid sirens. During a daylight raid on Grange aerodrome, we hadn't bothered even to take shelter under the table downstairs; in fact I was watching from our back bedroom window as the bombs 'tumbled down'. I had expected them to be a dull brown, as I had seen on many newsreels at the cinema, but to my surprise these were glistening silver.

Towards the end of the war, when the doodlebugs appeared upon the scene, our attitude to the hostilities definitely changed. Most people including myself considered these to be the most frightening of all the bombing episodes. Pat was on her way home from school one afternoon when the dreaded siren sounded. As she ran along Anglesea Road from the Raynes Road end, she heard the rough unmistakable motorbike sound of a doodlebug engine and she burst into tears of fear. Believe me, that sound really did strike fear into you. Suddenly she heard a voice calling out to her ... it was me. I had also heard the sound of the approaching flying bomb (to give it its correct title) and had taken shelter in the space underneath a brick water tank on the corner of Anglesea Road and Seymour Road. The tank was built on small brick support walls and it had a shallow void underneath, and a lot of fine rubble. I yelled at her to come and take cover. She quickly scrambled underneath the water tank with me and shortly after that the motorbike noise stopped. The silence was almost as bad as the sound of the engine. No, in truth it was even worse, because you knew that something unpleasant was going to happen very soon and very near. We heard the explosion, but it was not in the immediate vicinity and we sighed with relief.

My sister Pat

After the war it was acknowledged that on the night of 25 June 1944 a flying bomb had fallen on Stubbington and totally destroyed the picturesque buildings on the north side of the Green. This is just an illustration of how devastating the doodlebugs were – maybe not as bad as the aerial mines, but nonetheless bad enough.

Apart from the devastating attack on Daedalus in August 1940, only a few bombs were dropped on Lee-on-the-Solent: we did hear the thud of some that landed in the fields about 400 yards behind – that is to the north of – Brickland Terrace. Possibly they were jettisoned by some Luftwaffe aircrew trying to make their way back to the Fatherland. I have sometimes wondered if they all exploded. About a week later, when I was walking along the track across the fields, I saw some mounds where I had expected to see craters, because it was in the area where I thought that the bombs had landed. Although I had not been able to identify any bomb craters in the fields, I can say categorically that there was a crater in the promenade near where the Skate Park is now situated. I was cycling around the crater the day after the bomb had exploded there. As usual I was showing off, which always seems to be my downfall, and once again, downfall is a most apposite word. The bike slipped and I fell into the crater, landing on my back with the bike on top of me and I was still in the cycling position.

12

THE SOUND OF A DYING DUCK

During the war, church congregations were much larger than they are nowadays. For our family, like many others of various denominations, the church was quite an important part of our lives. I daresay that you probably think that I needed it, or that going to church didn't do me much good, in the light of my revelations (more to come). Irrespective of whichever of these was true, Mum, who was an ardent – more than devout – Catholic, took Pat and me to Mass every Sunday morning, and we were also sent to Catechism classes (Sunday school) in the afternoon. In addition to this there would often be a Benediction service in the evening. At that time, and indeed up to 1980, the Catholic Church at Lee consisted of an old asbestos shed-like building on the site of the present church in South Place.

Even though not all families went to church, practically all families tried to keep Sundays as a bit special, even if it was only for a bit of relaxation and peace and quiet. Allowing youngsters to play outside on Sundays was frowned upon most seriously, and the vast majority of parents would not let their children do it. In spite of this prevailing attitude, the parish priest at that time, who was very keen on football, would allow altar boys and other young lads of the parish to have a kick-about game of football in the back garden of the presbytery on some Sunday afternoons. This definitely did not meet with the approval of many parishioners, especially the ladies of the parish, my mum included. '*On a Sunday!*' was the oft-heard comment. And this was at a time when the Parish Priest was held in very high regard, and when criticising him was almost tantamount to blaspheming.

Except for going to church and Sunday school, Sundays were days when you did practically nothing, which meant that they were very, very, very long days indeed. A few people would go to the cinema at Lee Tower for the evening performance, but as it would be work the next day, and work started early, these performances drew quite small audiences.

During the 1940s and into the 1950s, it was the custom for some parishioners to have a seat in the church which they 'sponsored' and which had their name inserted in a holder at the front of the pew. It was 'their seat'. Our family finances did not run to this. So Mum, with Pat and me in tow, tended to be early for Mass, otherwise it meant a frantic scan to find three vacant seats next to each other.

When I was eleven, by which time we had a new parish priest, I was given instruction on how to serve on the altar. To be an acolyte in those days was somewhat different to what it is today. First and foremost, an altar- boy (it would be many decades before girls would be allowed on the altar) had to learn by heart long tracts of Latin.

This is how the Mass would proceed when there was just one altar boy. The priest, wearing his vestments and a biretta, a square cap with three flat projections (not a pistol!) would enter from the vestry, or 'changing room 'in lay parlance, and walk to the altar following the server. He would hand the biretta to the server, who would place it on a side table and then kneel on the opposite side to the priest. The altar was on the very back wall of the church (furthest from the entrance) and the priest and server for most of the Mass would have their backs to the congregation. The Latin responses had to be said clearly and loudly enough to be heard by the whole congregation. Other duties of the acolyte included moving the Mass book, from the Epistle-side of the altar to the Gospel side, after the Epistle, and then back to the Epistle-side after the Gospel. Also, the server had to hold a silver salver under the chins of parishioners as they knelt at the altar rail for communion.

Dad had recently become a Catholic. I am not sure if this was in some way connected with my eventually becoming a pupil at St John's

College in Southsea just under a year later. Shortly after I had started to serve on the altar, Dad was also taught how to serve at Mass by the parish priest. In return Dad tutored the priest in a rather different skill.

In addition to scavenging for ammunition and collecting shrapnel, I – like my contemporaries – also collected barrage balloon elastic, which came in the form of what could best be described as stretchy ropes of about half an inch in diameter and which were composed of about 50 sixteenth-of-an-inch square elastic strands.

To this day I have a lasting picture in my mind of Dad and the priest competing to kill flies at a range of about a yard with strands of this elastic by 'pinging them'. There did seem to be a lot more flies around then. Nevertheless it was quite an eye-opener to see the priest in a less ecclesiastical light.

In the church there was a harmonium which added a great deal of feeling and spiritual uplift to the Latin hymns during the Benedictions, but on other occasions I must admit that it was not quite so uplifting. There was a bit of a problem with the harmonium and the organist needed an assistant to lift some of the keys, which had a tendency to stick. On one notable occasion during a wedding, the assistant was either missing or rather slow in performing their task. The result was unintended musical variations which, for those who were attempting to sing the hymns, proved to be very tricky to follow; in fact the congregation failed miserably. The expression 'the sound of a dying duck' comes to mind.

13
A PINK TESTIMONIAL

With some help from our parish priest, the one who had studied 'fly swatting' with my father, I was accepted to be a pupil at St John's College Southsea. Mum Dad and I were collectively interviewed by the Brother Director. I must admit it felt more like an interrogation, probably because of my guilty conscience. Nevertheless I was accepted, and I started at the college in September 1943 in the Upper Third form. From then on I had to be careful not to get up to mischief, or at least not to get caught.

I enjoyed my time at St John's immensely. In the college there was a mixture of boarders and day-boys. I was a day-boy. From the very beginning it became apparent that this was to be a whole new experience. To start with, when writing in ink, I now had my own fountain pen; not as messy as the old pens, though it was still possible to get a little ink on unguarded fingers, especially if the top of the pen had not been screwed on properly after use. When I used my brand new 'Waterman' for the first time, I recalled my stained and strained introduction to writing with ink, five years previously. It had coincided with the introduction to the mysteries of that foreign language which was known as joined-up writing: how we had to copy into our books, over and over again, a letter of the alphabet as written on the blackboard by the teacher. No more of those comfortable capital letters. Once we had reached the letter 'z' we moved on to some two- and three-letter words. I had become 'fluent in the 'joined up' writing language, in fact I was now adding my own 'accent to the language' with my own flourishes. At St John's, classwork was far more rigorous and demanding, and there was always plenty of homework, with at least two subjects to be completed each night.

On every page of written work, in the top left-hand corner, we had to write the letters JMJ (Jesus, Mary, and Joseph). This illustrated the Catholic ethos that underpinned the teaching of the De La Salle Christian Brothers in St John's.

As well as Monday to Friday, we had to attend college for the first part of Saturday mornings. On these Saturday mornings all pupils were given a written testimonial for their week's performance, which took account of their classwork, homework, and behaviour. A pink testimonial was good, a blue one was fair, but a white one was poor. Three white testimonials in succession, and, the parents would be sent a letter, summoning them to visit the headmaster. In addition to the overall mark there was the position in the class, and these were read out.

I remember my first testimonial was a blue one and I was twenty-first in the class, the next week I had a pink testimonial and was fourteenth, the following week was pink again and I was seventh, and the week after that I was first, and stayed first or thereabouts for the rest of the year. At the end of that year I jumped a class and went from Upper Third to Upper Fourth, and started my ascent again, eventually reaching the number one spot. However, as luck would have it, despite continuing my good performance for two more years, when it came to the School Certificate examination I failed English language.

At St John's College there was a small contingent of pupils who travelled from Lee-on-the-Solent and Gosport and who, although of different ages and in different Forms, had some kind of collective identity. I often went to school with Denis Lazarus, whose family owned the 'Quick Turnover', a greengrocer's shop in Lee-on-the-Solent.

The journey to school was always interesting. We travelled by the Hants and Dorset bus from Lee to the Gosport Ferry, then the ferry across the harbour. I remember the names of three of the ferry-boats at that time, Vesta, Vadne, and the Venus. The captain would stand at the ship's wheel steering the ferry, in his pulpit-like bridge. His 'mate' and a deckhand were in charge of the hawsers that tied up the ferry, and the chains between the stanchions on the port side of the foredeck. The tying up of the ferry when it arrived at the pontoon was quite impressive to watch, especially if the sea was a bit rough. The hawser would be thrown, up to six feet, to lasso a bollard on the pontoon, and then deftly looped in a figure of eight around the pair of bollards on the foredeck to take the strain as the ferry tried to escape the restraining leash. It was a performance worthy of any wild-west rodeo show. Not until the ferry had been made fast would the chains be released by the captain and undone by the 'mate' or deckhand, and woe betide anyone else who had the temerity to try to undo the chains.

Embarking and disembarking at certain times of the day could be a pretty chaotic affair, with foot passengers vying with cyclists for the next position in the queue. The cycles were stacked on the foredeck against the chains on the opposite side to where the boarding took place. It was a system of 'last on first off'. The most hectic times were just after clocking-off in the dockyard. The vast majority of the dockyard employees owned bicycles and travelled to and from work on them. When it came to clocking-off, they emerged through the 'gates' like a swarm of angry bees coming out of a disturbed nest. Those cyclists who travelled across to Gosport on the ferry were in somewhat of a quandary, not wishing to miss the ferry but at the same time not wanting to be first on. If the sea was a bit rough it also meant that the bikes, especially those against the chains, were thoroughly dowsed with the spray.

Once we had disembarked on the Portsmouth side it was another bus or trolleybus ride. The number five trolleybus was the one that we would take if we had missed the bus to Elm Grove, because it went to South Parade pier with a stop at Handley's corner, which was near the present junction of Osborne Road and Palmerston Road, and not too much of a walk to the college. At 'The Hard' near the ferry, it was quite fascinating to watch when the conductor, with a long pole, changed the trolleybus connectors to a different line, for a 'return journey'.

The connectors consisted of two long parallel flexible poles, fixed on the top of the trolleybus. They protruded like an insect's antennae, and it was by means of these that the vehicles were connected to the electrical supply that was distributed by means of a series of pairs of overhead cables supported by tall poles along the various routes. There was a network of these cables spread like a giant cobweb above the streets of Portsmouth and Southsea. When the connectors were being changed to a different line, on most occasions it would be accompanied by a series of sparks, especially if it was raining.

On one cold, icy, finger-numbing winter's morning, as we were on our way to school, several of us had run down the slope to the pontoon on the Gosport side, attempting to catch the ferry before it cast off. The pontoon in those days had no cover or railings at the edge. There had been a heavy frost on this particular morning and it was very slippery underfoot. Although I had stopped running when I reached the pontoon, my momentum caused me to continue to slide and, in an instant, I could see the ominous threshed-up water between the ferryboat and the pontoon literally beneath my feet. As I was mentally preparing for the icy shock that I thought I was about to suffer, I could see and hear the propeller of the ferry that was thrashing away, straining to keep the stern of the ferry close to the jetty, just a few feet from where I thought I was about to enter the water. I had both feet on the narrow metal strip at the edge of the pontoon, when Denis grabbed hold of me by my satchel. Although I was quite a good swimmer, I was wearing heavy winter clothes, and

The Gosport Ferry

had a satchel heavy with books over my shoulder. Dennis was much heavier than I was, and he brought me to an abrupt stop. I took a rapid step back from the brink. I believed then, and still do, that he most probably saved my life that day.

Apparently when he got home that evening and his parents asked him about his day he just said: '*oh I stopped John Green from getting wet.*'

Travelling to school was sometimes fun. In the winter we would often go downstairs ('down below') and stand in a passageway alongside the boiler room by the open door and watch as the stoker shovelled coal into the boiler. It was warm and was a good place to dry out if you had got wet. It had a particular welcoming smell of coal and hot oil.

On a few occasions when there was dense fog, and there were certainly more fogs in the late 40s and early 50s, although the normal ferry would not run because of the reduced visibility, the Floating Bridge car ferry which operated on a fixed chain would continue plying between Gosport and Portsmouth. Instead of waiting for the normal ferry and arriving late, we would travel on the car ferry as foot passengers to get to school. This ferry operated from about where the Harbour Tower flats are situated into the Old Portsmouth harbour near the Still and West public house.

The old Floating Bridge car ferry

14

D-DAY: BEFORE AND AFTER

In the build-up for D-Day, thousands of soldiers mustered throughout the area in numerous locations. As part of this, soldiers from the USA, Canada and the UK were based on the cliff-lands in Lee-on-the-Solent, most of them under canvas. Broadly speaking, the Canadians were encamped at the eastern end of the cliff-lands near where the present sailing club is situated, the Americans had set up camp to the west of Lee Tower, and the British troops were on the cliff-lands between Beach Road and Cambridge Road.

The Americans were known for chewing gum, Camel and Lucky Strike cigarettes and most of all for nylons. It was to be some time before many synthetic materials were to be discovered, but nylon as a material was just beginning to be produced, and most importantly for the ladies, nylon stockings appeared on the scene, but with only a limited availability. Although wearing them also involved the wearing of a suspender belt (I am told), nylons became much sought-after items, and it was rumoured that the Americans used them as a means of bartering with young and not-so-young ladies for their favours. Although the name is supposedly derived from the two places where it was developed – New York and London -the 'poor British Tommy' didn't have any nylons available to assist him in his cause, and had to rely upon his natural charms.

Later I was to learn from my wife and sister that the more mature ladies had a preference for rayon stockings, which were not as sheer as nylons. The Americans were not the only source of nylon stockings, because some young men who lived in the area, who were in the Merchant Navy and were fortunate enough to be on the ships that went to and fro between the UK and the USA (if you can call running the gauntlet of the U-boat wolf packs luck), were able to lay their hands on supplies. However, their motive was more mercenary than amorous: they would buy them in America relatively cheaply and sell them for one pound a pair, a substantial profit and a lot of money at that time. It would have been about a day's wages for many young women.

The first nylon stockings had a seam at the back, and according to my wife and sister, it was not easy to keep the seam straight when putting on the stocking. Young ladies who didn't own a pair of nylons would resort to 'painting' their legs with light brown water-based paint and then they would draw a line with a dark crayon where the seam should be. The fortunate young ladies who did own a pair of nylons (no awkward questions as to how they came by them) treasured them and took great care not to ladder them. As an added precaution, whenever they went out they would carry a small bottle of clear nail varnish in their handbag. If they did have the misfortune to snag their treasured items, they would apply a small dab of the varnish to the snag to stop the ladder from 'running'. There were even establishments that repaired nylons. One of these was the Silver Arrow laundry and cleaners on the corner of North Cross Street and High Street in Gosport.

Let me assure you that this information about ladies laddering their nylons is completely secondhand ... well, more or less.

When the troops were assembling for D-Day, although the beach was cordoned off with barbed wire, the troops under canvas on the cliffs had surprisingly little security, and as remarkable as it may seem, it was possible for us youngsters to walk among the assembled tents. In fact, during a period just after D-Day, when the army still had a large marquee on the cliffs opposite the Bellevue Hotel, any youngsters who happened to be in the area were invited into the marquee and treated to tea (sweetened with condensed milk) and buns by a small contingent of troops who were probably waiting to be shipped to Normandy. It may not sound much, but it was greatly appreciated by all of us who were fortunate enough to have been there.

Now that I was a pupil at St John's, I lost touch with many of the lads that I had associated with previously. We gradually drifted apart, not intentionally or by design, but because we were being subjected to different sets of experiences. It was just before D-Day when I had happened to meet up with two lads from the past, one of them an older brother of Ronnie, and somehow we had managed to get on the beach at the western end of Stokes Bay. We were just standing on a grassy patch near the beach, and I suppose we were trying to blend into the background of shrubs and trees as we casually watched DUKWs (Ducks) and tanks being loaded onto landing craft.

It was an absolute hive of activity, and we thought that we were quite inconspicuous where we were, but no! We were seen by one of the officers, who became agitated, and that is putting it mildly. He promptly had us 'escorted' to the road under armed guard.

The military vehicles that we had just observed being loaded on to the landing craft had, for a number of weeks, been 'hidden' in the grounds of what is now Bay House School. When I say hidden, that is only partly correct because they could be seen quite clearly from the top of any bus en route between Lee-on-the-Solent and Gosport, and although all of this military hardware disappeared soon after D-Day, the large number of caterpillar-tracked army vehicles such as tanks and Bren-gun carriers had played havoc with many of the kerbstones in the area, and this damage was a testament to their having been here. It remained a reminder for many years after the war.

During the war there was an army checkpoint on the corner of Gomer Lane and Browndown Road, which at that time was a military road. The corner was in fact a T-junction if you included the track that led into Stokes Bay. All vehicles were stopped at this checkpoint and all occupants of the vehicles were checked. On one occasion when I was among the passengers travelling on the bus to Lee from Gosport, as usual it was stopped, everyone had to disembark and wait in a queue to have their identity cards checked before being allowed back onto the bus. Identity cards had to be carried at all times. There were several of us young lads who had ended up at the back of the queue – this was quite customary because everyone knew their place. Unfortunately for us, we didn't manage to get back onto the bus before it set off again. Consequently we had to walk from there to Lee. Not that this was any great hardship, but we felt quite aggrieved because we had paid our fares.

One afternoon about a week or so after D-Day, I was cycling along Privett Road on my way home from St John's College. On the other side of the road was a column of about a dozen large mobile long-barrelled guns together with a number of trucks. Some of the soldiers called out to me: '*Hey lad! Can you go and get us some bread?*' I stopped and crossed the road and they gave me some money, asking me to go and get whatever I could. So I turned round and cycled back to a baker's, near the White Hart, and bought as much bread as I could carry. It must have been more than half a dozen loaves. I didn't need coupons, because bread rationing didn't come into force until later. When I got back and gave the soldiers the bread and their change they were delighted, and were obviously very hungry. For doing the errand they offered me money – half a crown, which was a lot of money, and it would have paid for quite a few visits to the cinema, but I said no thank you and that I didn't want to be paid. What I did say was: '*I wouldn't mind one of those,*' pointing to what turned out to be occupation money that I had seen one of them had in his wallet. I remember the soldier who gave me one of the notes saying jokingly: '*Look he doesn't want what's no use to us and he's taking money we could spend tomorrow.*' They gave me a five franc note, worth a few pence then, but that note has become one of my most treasured possessions which I still have seventy years later.

After D-Day it became easier to get onto the beach, where our 'scavenging' became directed at a different target: we became beachcombers and the coveted prizes that we were looking for were K rations and D rations. They were packets that measured about 8 inches by 4 inches by 2 inches and were encased in semi-waterproof packaging – a kind of waxy thick paper. These 'rations', we discovered later, were a day's supply issued to soldiers when they were fighting at

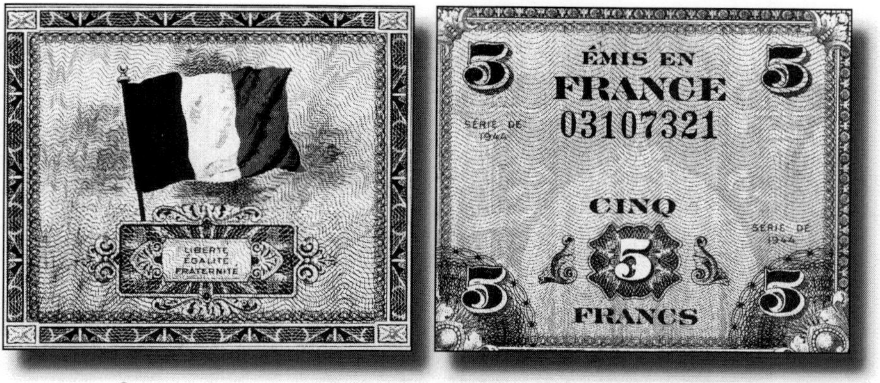

Five franc note issued to soldiers – one of my most treasured possessions

the frontline and were unable to get to a feeding station. These K and D rations were flotsam produced when military vessels were sunk, most likely on the other side of the channel, and it must have taken quite a while before the tides and waves washed them on to the foreshore at Lee-on-the-Solent. These coveted finds contained, among other things, sachets of coffee, biscuits, sweets which were a bit like glucose tablets, and cigarettes. The K rations were for American troops and the D rations were for British troops. The outside of the packets was often coated with tar, but the contents in many cases were still intact. On one beachcombing day a group of us found the remains of a large package which had contained about a hundred D rations: there was still about three quarters of it intact. On another day I found a case of lard which weighed about 10lbs: as the weekly ration per person was two ounces, Mum was very pleased with this find, even though only about a quarter of it was useable.

At the end of the war in Europe, there were great celebrations. Everyone who was around at that time will remember the VE celebrations. Nearly every road had its own street party. The party for our immediate area was held in our garage. Well, it was not really a garage because we – like most people in Elmore – had no car. The bikes and tools were moved out, the walls and floor were washed down, and tables from various houses were set in the middle with sheets for tablecloths. I cannot remember what the food was, but I remember that it was a most enjoyable occasion. It always seems incredible that, in times of necessity, mothers seem to be able to conjure surprises out of nowhere.

Although there had not been any air-raids for a long time, it was not until after VE Day that people no longer had to bother about the blackout. With the restrictions removed, lights were put on and the curtains and blackout were not pulled. The criss-crossed sticky tape was taken from the windows.

In May 1945 there was a Victory party put on by the combined personnel of HMS Daedalus for all of the local children. The party was held in the ballroom at Lee Tower and there was, what seemed to me and the other children present, a huge spread. We were all given, among other things, a commemorative victory spoon as a memento.

15
THE MONSTER IN THE BATHROOM

Death and taxes may always be with us but so is change, and this became dramatically apparent after the war, when the pace of changed greatly increased. It was as if the Almighty had suddenly decided to put his foot down on the accelerator of life in general, and my life in particular. What we considered to be our 'village' was about to undergo a series of growing pains, changing from being a village of two halves to a town of two halves. The harbinger of this change was the arrival of the prefabs. Several dozen of them were erected on the land behind Gosport Road and Brickland Terrace, on what previously had been farmland.

This was in the spring of 1946, when all and sundry – wives, mothers, and children – stood in the road outside their houses to watch with awe at the arrival of the ready-made homes being transported-in on large trailers hauled by lorries, to the sites of previously prepared foundations, which lined a few extra concrete roads that had been built in the fields nearby. The prefabs had arrived! Throughout the land prefab estates had spread far and wide, like a rash, to replace housing destroyed during the war. Although there had been very little destruction in Lee-on-the-Solent, here were some of them arriving in our own little 'patch'. One particular feature that was enviously observed in these clean and fresh-looking pale-green-and-cream little buildings (which came in four parts with their ready built insides of kitchen and bathrooms) was the fact that the prefabs had fridges! This was before fridges became commonplace: not many houses, especially those in Elmore, would have had that luxury. In fact, you would have been able to count on the fingers of one hand the number of houses in our area that had a fridge.

Mum was very house-proud, and she kept the place spick and span – in fact everyone had to take their shoes off at the door when they came in. Although the house was only about ten years old and kept in pristine condition by Mum, we certainly didn't have a fridge, washing machine, tumble drier, dishwasher or central heating.

In our house, as with most of the houses in Elmore, there were only cold-water taps. We had one in the kitchen, and two in the bathroom. If Mum wanted hot water in the kitchen it meant filling a kettle and putting it on the gas stove. As for hot water for a bath, that was a different kettle of fish, so to speak. It involved using the geyser above the bath. Geysers were 'fearsome beasts' – well, the one in our bathroom certainly was. To light it meant using a lit taper or, more often than not, a small rolled-up piece of newspaper. The gas to the appliance had to be turned on and then the 'flaming brand' had to be inserted through a small aperture into the 'innards' of the beast ... and then there was a minor explosion as the burners lit. Lighting 'the monster in the bathroom' was always a nerve-racking experience, because the longer it took to light it, the greater the explosion would be. Mother dreaded lighting it; in fact when Dad was not at home, we would often make do with a wash-down in the kitchen sink, with hot water supplied courtesy of the kettle. Fortunately Mum didn't have so much trouble lighting the appliance in which she washed the clothes. It was a gas 'copper', as the clothes boilers were known. It had a long flexible hose, and when she wanted to use the 'copper', she would connect it to a designated gas tap in the kitchen. The rather ugly little grey thing with four short bow legs would sit sulking in the corner of the kitchen between washdays. That is, until 1949, when Dad decided that it was time to replace the coal fires downstairs with modern (state-of-the-art) gas fires.

Our front room

This meant, as we no longer required a coal shed, it became home for the 'copper'. Every Monday it would be dragged out and set to work by Mum. On fine days this would take place on the concrete hard-standing outside the kitchen, and on wet days inside the kitchen, where it would wreak its revenge for being locked in the 'coal hole 'by filling the kitchen with steam. As a companion for the copper we had a large mangle with wooden rollers, on the opposite side of the concrete base at the back of the house.

Up to the late 1950s a number of roads in Lee-on-the-Solent, particularly in Elmore, were 'unadopted', that is that they had not been taken over by Gosport Borough Council for maintenance, so were not covered with concrete or tarmac. Effectively this meant that they were not much better than dirt roads – often full of potholes, and without pavements. When it rained, these roads became overwhelmed with puddles and it was impossible to walk dry-shod between the puddles. As we lived on a corner house we found it particularly difficult, especially as the worst-affected of the roads were Anglesea Road,

Wootton Road, and Gosport Road as far as Cross Road. This placed us in the middle of the 'near impassable roads zone'.

After the war ended and the pace of change seemed to accelerate, more and more of what had been our playgrounds, the green spaces between the houses and bungalows disappeared, as did some of the surrounding farmland. Along with my contemporaries, I was beginning to grow out of play escapism so I did not feel the loss too much. Nevertheless eventually all of the 'Greens' became covered with bungalows and houses and the 'gaps' in Gosport Road and Wootton Road and the bottom of Raynes Road were built upon.

Mum and Dad in the garden
(note the street gaslight in the background)

At the same time as the play areas were disappearing, the roads began to be adopted and covered with tarmac or concrete; also pavements were built. Apart from making the roadways narrower, another downside to this for the owners of the properties abutting the roads, was that they had to pay for the work involved. Because Dad had bought our house, which was on a corner, it proved to be quite a heavy financial burden. The main upside was the fact that it was now possible to walk along the roads after it had rained.

At the same that this time was happening, the street lighting was being changed over to electricity. Although gas lamps may conjure up a picture of Victorian England, even as late as the 1950s, street lighting in Lee-on-the-Solent was by means of gas lamps. In addition to not being very bright, the lamps were very few and far between. Although they were not lit during the war years, once hostilities were over they were brought back into operation and a man came round at dusk to light them. I remember seeing this. He must have made a second visit later to turn them off, probably just after midnight, although I never actually saw it being done. There was one on the corner of Anglesea Road and Gosport Road, and another outside the pig farm at the bottom of Wootton Road.

During the hours of darkness when the gas street lights had been lit, and when there was little or no moonlight, youngsters – myself included – would run between the pools of light from these street lights; they were the circles of safety providing sanctuary from the imagined monsters lurking menacingly in the blackness. It was noticeable that even adults appeared to quicken their pace between the illuminated patches.

Before the roads became adopted, if rain and puddles had made it impossible to walk in the middle of the road as we normally did (cars were rarely encountered), we had to walk along the edges of the road, and this was the absolute worst situation. On these occasions the darkness seemed even more intense and the imagined monsters even more malevolent, with the shrubbery at the side of the road seeming to reach out to grab passersby.

16

HANGOUTS

Despite the occasional scary walk home during the dark winter nights, I was very much the Lone Ranger without a Tonto, and I would spend hours on my own in Lee public library, most times staying until closing. My favourite was reading encyclopaediae in the junior reference section. In those days the silence rule was rigorously enforced and everyone spoke with hushed voices when checking in and checking out their books. Once you were in the library, you didn't speak at all.

The children's section was in the front of the library on the west side with the 'newspaper room' at the front on the east side, and the main (adult) library taking up most of the rest of the lower floor of the building. During the war there was a temporary office alongside the newspaper room, where mothers would go at strictly regulated times, 'Two o'clock till three o'clock', with their families to collect free bottles of very concentrated orange juice and rosehip syrup. The bottles were about the size of a medicine bottle and the contents tasted a lot like medicine.

Throughout the war and after, Lee Tower was the absolute focus of life in Lee-on-the-Solent. When making arrangements, the most frequently heard phrase was '*see you up the Tower*'. This didn't actually mean at the top of the Tower, but somewhere in the vicinity of the complex.

The cinema was on the east side of the building and it had a Circle and Stalls, and between the two levels, there was a short stairway on either side. It was not unknown for youngsters – yes, including me – to pay to go downstairs and then to sneak up one of the stairways, most times to get caught by an usherette, and either sent back down or sent out of the cinema. On Saturday mornings it was threepence for downstairs, and sixpence for upstairs. For that princely sum, normally there would be two films, one or two cartoons and maybe a Pathé News. The prices were significantly dearer in the evening: a shilling in the stalls, and 1s 9d in the circle. The films were changed every Monday, Thursday, and Sunday. That is six different films plus the Saturday morning matinee, and the Pearl and Deane trailers and advertisements. Mr and Mrs Rogers, who had two daughters and lived in Wootton Road, could be seen almost every Sunday, Monday and Thursday evening walking past our house and down Gosport Road on their way to the cinema.

Lee Tower

On the west side of Lee Tower building was the ballroom which, during the war, was also used as a gymnasium by the Fleet Air Arm. After the war it reverted to being a ballroom, and the Bert Sharpe Band became one of the long-term resident bands. Before we were old enough to go into the ballroom, I, together with other youngsters, would often gather behind the Tower on Saturday evenings and peep enviously into the ballroom through any gaps that had been left in the curtains. My sister later said that when she was old enough to go to dances, she would on occasion, when 'sitting out a dance', look out through similar gaps. She said it was quite educational because young sailors with young ladies outside were totally unaware that they could be seen getting up to what they were 'getting up to'.

The Tower itself had a lift or stairs to the top. It was 3d 'thrupence' to enter. A few years earlier, when I was younger, the trick used to gain a free trip to the top was to wait until the lift had begun to ascend with the customers and attendant in it, then to nip under the barrier, onto the stairway and run up. We would wait at the point where the stairs coincided with the back of the lift, until the lift was on its way down again –once it had passed – we would run to the top. Getting down was a bit trickier, especially if business was not too brisk.

Although growing up in the 40s and 50s in Lee-on-the-Solent meant that the Tower was always the main assembly point, another important meeting venue, especially for teenagers, was the Bluebird Café on the corner of Milvil Road and Marine Parade opposite the Tower. Basically it was a hut with a veranda and – most importantly – a jukebox. My favourite record, in 1949 was 'Ghost Riders in the Sky' sung by Frankie Laine. But on one occasion, after I had played it twice in succession, I had to beat a hasty retreat when I went to play it a third time.[2]

The Amusement Arcade was also a Mecca for young people, especially in the summer. Originally the building had been the railway station booking office and waiting room, until the line was closed in the early 30s. Now, two decades later, it enjoyed a revival as a 'hang out'.

Between the Tower and the row of shops and flats on Marine Parade were the remembrance gardens, with the memorial to the fallen in the centre. These gardens were cupped by a semicircular one-way road that the buses to Gosport and Fareham would pull into and stop in front of the Tower. The Fareham buses, mostly

2 www.en.wikipedia.org/wiki/(Ghost)_Riders_in_the_Sky:_A_Cowboy_Legend

single-deckers, would stop on the eastern section of the semicircular road and the Gosport buses, mainly double-deckers, would stop on the western section.

As a general rule we would walk to and from Lee Tower, but when we wanted to use the bus to get home from the cinema, if we had just missed one and it was pulling away from the bus stop, we would run through Pier Street, and although there was two-way traffic in the High Street, invariably we would manage to catch the bus at the stop at the junction of Pier Street and High Street.

The area of the library was another focal point for social activity, particularly for the adults in Lee. Opposite the library was the Lowry Hall, which was always known as the Lowry Hut, and which was used by the Women's Institute, British Legion and other institutions. Also there were many functions held there such as whist drives, jumble sales, and concerts. A very popular tap-dance group of girls from Gosport, the 'Sunshine Kiddies' whose ages ranged from about seven to fourteen, occasionally put on a performance at the Lowry Hut.

Not far from the library, on the same side of the road, was the Police Station, which continued to be located there until the 1960s. During the war, much of the constabulary's time was taken up with catching people who were contravening blackout regulations or cycling without lights ... or they were chasing after young miscreants.

17

A BIT OF LIBERATING

HMS Daedalus as a military establishment had a large bearing on the lives of the people in Lee-on-the-Solent, including our family. Apart from it being a target for the German Luftwaffe during the war, it was a source of employment. It also put the town firmly on the map with its annual Air Display which always attracted many visitors, and brought in a lot of trade as well as providing advertising for the 'resort'. But the Air Displays didn't always go to plan: in 1947 there was a bad air-crash, as was reported in the press at the time.

> ***July 1947...*** *Inquest on the air-show crash. The Pilot was warned not to do any aerobatics, but in spite of that, he attempted to do a roll and crashed. He was told to carry out a fly past to demonstrate a Blackburn Firebrand carrying a torpedo. After taking off he came over the aerodrome at about 50 ft and when at the Eastern end pulled up to about 200 ft and started to execute a roll. While in the inverted position he started to lose height there appeared to be an attempt to right the aircraft and it disappeared from view. He was single and 22.*

There was a sequel to this. Brian's dad worked in a telephone exchange at the then top end of Manor Way, near the present-day junction with Cheltenham Crescent. On the day of the air show he came home somewhat distressed and needed to take a few days off work.

Brian told me some time later in a quiet voice, almost a whisper as if it was some family secret, that his dad had heard the crash on that day, and had gone out of the telephone bunker. Not far from the exchange he saw what he thought was the pilot's helmet, not the hard shiny type of today, but soft brown leather headgear. When he bent down to pick it up, he discovered that the unfortunate pilot's head was still in the helmet.

Although Dad had been posted away on a few occasions during the war, for the majority of his time in the Fleet Air Arm he was based in Daedalus. In the summer of 1946 he was a CPO in charge of quite a large team of young sailors that worked mainly on the servicing Swordfish aircraft. Somehow he had managed to arrange for me to go into Daedalus on a few Saturdays when I was not at school. On these visits I began to learn a lot about the Swordfish aircraft, and what life was like for the young Fleet Air Arm mechanics.

At the end of each Saturday's duty, he would let two of his team have a forty-eight hour pass for the following weekend. On one of these Saturday mornings, when I had been allowed to accompany Dad onto the base, there must have been something special going on the following weekend, because the young servicemen seemed to be very keen to please 'Chief', as they called him and – in order to curry favour with him – two of them even let me put a repair patch on one of the planes.

The Swordfish or 'Stringbag' was made of a wooden frame with material stretched over it, and this meant that it was quite easy to accidentally damage the 'skin', which generally would be repaired with a patch of the same silver coloured material, 'glued on' with 'dope'. At the end of the day Dad asked me who should get the passes. Obviously I chose the two who had let me do the repair.

'Acquired' items on a military establishment which found their way into civilian houses were known as 'Rabbits' – there were even cartoons about this in the local press. I wonder if they were they called Rabbits because they had burrowed their way out? There was a saying at that time, 'if all the Rabbits that had come out of Portsmouth dockyard were to be returned, half of the houses in Portsmouth would fall down'. This, although anecdotal, gives some idea of how widespread the petty pilfering was. Of course this was at a time when there were virtually no places where you could easily get materials.

Over the garden fence – Mum, Herb and Hilda

Dad, ever resourceful and generally honest, hated to see anything being wasted, and if material was to be thrown away or destroyed he would find a use for it and 'liberate' it. Later that summer on a weekday, when again I had been allowed to go in with Dad, the following little incident took place. Earlier that week he had come across some small pieces of hardwood that were to be thrown away and which he decided would be useful for a for a job at home that he had in mind, so he had 'liberated' them and put them in a safe place. At midday Dad and I were just about to wheel our bikes out of the Daedalus main gate to make our way home for lunch, with the 'Rabbits' in his saddlebag. He told me to hold his bike and wait while he had a word with one of policemen on the gate that he knew. Apparently he said to him that he had seen some wood in the hangar and asked if would be alright to take it out that evening. The policeman said *'That'll be alright Jack'* (although my dad's name was John, he was always called Jack or Jimmy or Bill). We went through the gates and cycled home. That evening when Dad came out of the gate, he was called into the gatehouse and he and his bike were searched … .too late of course – he already had the wood at home. He just told them that he had changed his mind.

In 1947, when I was fifteen, I was able to join the gym club at school. It was something that I greatly enjoyed and I discovered that I had a very good sense of balance and excelled on the parallel bars. Within a year I was awarded my gym colours and eventually became vice captain of the team. We were quite a strong team and in a competition against the Army Gymnastics Team at Aldershot, we gave them a jolly good run for their money..

Gym club: I am in the front row, third from the right

Armed with the confidence that I had gained during the frequent gym club sessions, and seasoned with a wish to show off, I 'demonstrated' on a number of occasions an outward-facing handstand on the handrail at the top of the steps behind the ballroom at the back of the Tower. It was a drop of about twenty feet. Although I claimed that it was the exuberance and the confidence of youth, if I am truthful, I have to admit that I was just showing off. Another favourite 'showing off' activity, for some of us, was sprinting across the promenade just to the east of the Tower and launching ourselves into the air onto the shingle beach, using the sloping shingle to break our fall. One day a passerby even asked us to repeat the jump so that he could take a photograph of us. It may have looked quite spectacular, but it was only a drop of about seven feet, so it was small fry compared to the gang entrance requirement down at Elmore a few years earlier.

On the seafront where Chaplin's restaurant now stands was a seawater swimming pool, which was about 240 feet long. In summer of 1945, I held the record for swimming the fastest length, as timed by the swimming pool attendant. But it was a briefly held record: within half an hour it was taken from me by Peter Brown who had, with his parents, lived in South Africa for some time, and he was an excellent swimmer. He was a few years older than me and in fact at one time had been my swimming mentor. He took two seconds off my temporary record, and that put me in my place. When the tide was low or the sea was too rough we tended to use the swimming pool, but at other times it would be quite a lonely place.

It was during this summer that a German prisoner of war taught some of us lads how to dive. The prisoners had large yellow patches sewn into the backs of their clothes, but they were allowed to walk unaccompanied between where they worked on the land or building sites and where they were to be 'locked up' for the night. This particular prisoner would stop for a swim at the swimming pool on his way back to Stubbington. Somehow we got talking to him, probably just out of curiosity: this was the first German that we had met face to face. He told us that he came from Leipzig and he was quite well accepted, but it was not really the done thing to like the Germans at that time. Interestingly, there were quite a few German prisoners of war housed and working in the area who were involved with the building of the new Bridgemary estate. Anyhow, this prisoner of war could see that we were having difficulty with diving, and he offered to help us. Looking back I realise that he was very authoritarian, which of course is an alleged Teutonic trait. Nevertheless, when he commanded '*Don't look at the water! It will still be there when you get there!*' and then when he said '*Dive!*' we obeyed instantly and instinctively and learned to dive pretty well. We were taught to do jack knives and swallow dives, from what must have been a six-feet board. Later we even ventured to dive from what must have been a fifteen-feet board.

Within about a year of the diving lessons, the diving boards were removed, the pool was shortened and the deep end was partly filled in and made into a kiddies' pool; later it was completely filled in.

Although I represented the school in swimming and gymnastics, I was no athlete, but that summer turned out to be quite fruitful for me at a sports day put on by the personnel from Daedalus in their sports field. This venue was opposite the Tennis Club in Manor Way, and was bounded by tall trees adjacent to the road. I teamed up with a girl called Beryl, who was one of three girls fostered-out in the same house in Seymour Road. We were remarkably successful in all of the races including the wheelbarrow race, the three-legged race, and many others. It was almost embarrassing the number of prizes which we won … well almost, but then again, perhaps not. I think that we won all but one race.

At this Sports Day there was also a Baby Show at which soft toys were presented as prizes and these had been made by Dad.

A press report at the time stated: '*the civilian staff of HMS Daedalus held sports fete in the grounds of Edinburgh House. The prizes for the baby show were kindly given by C.P.O. Green … they were toy Elephants.*'

This brought back memories for my sister and she recalled the toy elephants that Dad had made for her a few years previously.

18

STOP ME AND BUY ONE

In the summer of 1948 I managed to get a number of different jobs. In the High Street towards the east end was Browning's, the baker's, the proprietors of which had tragically lost their son in the raid on Daedalus 16 August 1940. In addition to the bakery they also had franchises for selling ice cream at Lee, Stokes Bay and Bridgemary – this I know because that summer I worked for them selling ice cream from a tricycle. I joined the ranks of what were known as 'stop me and buy one' ice cream men.

On one of my days off, I was among a gathering of young chaps who had swum out to the end of the remains of the pier. It was an impromptu gathering – some of the group I knew but there were others who were complete strangers to me. As the tide had dropped quite a bit while we were on the jetty just 'chilling out', a collective decision was made not to swim back to the beach. Instead we set about walking along the tops of the girders to the beach, and where there were gaps in the ironwork we swung hand-over-hand along a one-inch wire hawser that stretched from the Tower to the end of the pier, in line with the top of the girders. Unfortunately there was a problem with this, as we soon discovered. The hawser cut our hands to pieces as we made our way across the gaps. We all persevered and managed to get to the last intact piece of girder and climb down, but needless to say none of us ever tried that again.

Not exactly a summer of painful experiences, but there was a second incident a couple of weeks later. On this occasion Vic Newman, a friend from school and fellow gym club member, who lived in Fareham, came to Lee for the day and we met up near the Tower to go for a swim. Although it was low tide we decided we would still go in for a dip. We were on the beach near the Amusement Arcade and Vic, who liked to run into the sea, ran down the beach and splashed through the shallow water. Normally we only swam in that area when the tide was high and we didn't know that there was a mussel-bed near the pier which Vic ran straight across; his feet were extremely badly lacerated and there was blood everywhere. However, with the help of another person on the beach I managed to get him to the St John's Ambulance hut, which was near where the Skate Park is now situated. They bandaged his feet and he managed to hobble home with me. It goes without saying that we never tried swimming near the pier again at low tide.

Another job that I had in 1948 and 1949 was as an errand boy in Beaney's grocery shop. It was more like a delicatessen, and later it changed ownership and became Hearn's. The shop was a few doors along from the Hove-To tearooms. I got on very well with Mr and Mrs Beaney. Among the things that I was allowed to do, when not out delivering groceries, was to stack the shelves behind the counter and along one wall, and I was also permitted to grind the coffee. One day they both asked if I would like to learn the business if I didn't go in the RAF. They also said that, if I came to work for them full-time, they would teach me the business and how to drive the shop's van. This was not really a feasible option for me, because I was aware that I would have to do my National Service if I chose not to sign up. In addition, the grocery trade was not for me: I couldn't see myself as a budding Sir Thomas Lipton.

In the winter on Sunday mornings after early church, I worked in the Browning's crumpet factory as a 'ring greaser'. The factory was just off Grove Road. Although it involved working with bare arms, it was a good job to have in the winter because it was in a very warm environment. In fact it was very hot work. In the bakery-cum-factory there were a series of large hotplates in a line. Each hotplate measured about five feet by two-and-a-half feet, and they were about three feet from the floor. My job consisted of setting out in rows onto the hotplate a series of pre-greased metal rings. They were about three-inches in diameter and three-quarter-of-an-inch deep. To grease them

I first slid about half a dozen of the rings up my bare left arm (the task could only be performed by someone with slim arms) then – taking care to keep the rings on my arm – I'd pick up a piece of sacking which looked rather like a dirty old tea-towel. Holding it by each end with both hands, with an up-and-down movement I'd dunk it in a bucket on the floor held between my feet, which contained some mucky-looking translucent cooking oil/grease. Where I went, that bucket went. Then, with circular twirling movements of the sacking in front of me I'd transfer the rings from my left arm to my right, in the process coating the rings with the lubricant. Next I would drop the sacking into the bucket and set the rings out on the hotplate in neat rows, using my left hand. The first batch was the easiest because the rings were taken (cold) from a box. Starting on the left, I laid out rows across the hotplate. When I reached the end of the series of hotplates, I went back to the beginning with my bucket and piece of sacking. And this is where it got tricky, because the baker followed behind me and poured the crumpet mixture into the rings as soon as I'd set them out and when he considered the crumpets to be correctly cooked, he went along the hotplate and turned the crumpets out, leaving the rings on the hot surface in irregular piles. Now it was ooch-ouch time as I started the process all over again, but this time with rings that varied from being very warm to ruddy hot.

As my schooldays were coming to an end, I thought it would be a good idea if I was able to get some understanding of radios, as I had decided that was the kind of thing that I would like to be involved with in the RAF. To this end I approached the owner of a radio shop on the corner of Elmore Road and Gosport Road. He said that I could help out at the back of the shop on Saturdays, but it would be unpaid work.

Although the shop sold radios, it was mainly a place where people took their radios for repair, or their accumulators for charging. I helped out in the shop for a few months, and I learnt the names of a few of the pieces inside the magical boxes.

Many of the radios at that time were powered by batteries. Typically a radio would require a high-tension battery which measured about 12" x 6" x 4", and an accumulator (rechargeable battery) which had a rectangular glass case and which measured about 4"x 4" x 8". These two items made the radios very bulky. The accumulator was needed to provide the low-tension supply (low voltage) for the filaments of the valves, and these accumulators had to be charged-up every few weeks or so. The large battery was needed for the rest of the functions of the apparatus. All wirelesses needed to be connected to a substantial aerial: a small piece of wire hanging out the back of the apparatus would have been as much use as the proverbial 'back pocket in a vest'. Although I was not paid for working in the shop, the owner occasionally gave me bits and pieces of broken equipment to take home to tinker about with. Of the pieces of broken equipment that I was given, the one that I remember most vividly was a defunct high tension supply. People bought these pieces of equipment so that they would not have to keep replacing the large HT batteries, which were not rechargeable and had to be replaced at fairly regular intervals.

Anyhow, I proudly took home my HT supply, even if it didn't work, and that evening, in my bedroom I plugged it in. It glowed as its valves warmed up, then the glow changed to an eerie blue, as if a scene from a Frankenstein film were about to be re-enacted. Even with my brief acquaintance with radios and their valves, I knew that they were not supposed to do that. Unfortunately my recently acquired treasure, as it sat on my tallboy, glowing with its eerie blue light, was creating havoc with local radio reception. It caused all of the wirelesses in the area to whistle and howl, and what was particularly unfortunate was that it happened just at the time when the football results were being read out. This was when dreams of becoming rich were based on winning the football pools. Visualise what the reaction today would be, if during the programme when the numbered Lotto balls were rolling out of the machine, all TV screens suddenly went blank. Well on that day, as a result of me switching on my HT supply, there were a number of very irate men in the houses roundabout, including my Dad. I said nothing. Fortunately they didn't know that I was the culprit.

19

FOLLOWING MY DEAR OLD DAD

So here I was, not exactly fully appraised of the 'facts of life', but I had survived the 'man to man talk' and was about to set out on that journey where quite a few had gone before. I was eager and ready to go. I was about to start living apart from the bosom of my family.

Just about to set out

Because, unlike most applicants, I had passed the School Certificate Exam and had not been required to take the apprentice entrance exam, I was what was known as a Direct Entry. When all us aspiring apprentices had attended the assessment session at RAF Hornchurch a couple of days previously, the Selection Board had decided that I would be suitable material to train as a Radio Fitter at the RAF Apprentice School at Cranwell.

On 8 June 1949, I was among the accepted candidates who swore the oath of allegiance. In unison, with each saying their name at the appropriate time, we all said:

'I, ………, swear by almighty God that I will be faithful and bear true allegiance to his Majesty King George the Sixth, his Heirs and Successors, and that I will, in duty bound, honestly and faithfully defend His Majesty His Heirs and Successors, in Person, Crown and Dignity against all enemies and will observe and obey all orders of His Majesty, His Heirs and Successors and of All the Air Officers and Officers set over me. SO HELP ME GOD.'

I had 'taken the King's shilling' and agreed to serve 'the Crown' for the next twelve years after reaching my eighteenth birthday. This was the day on which I considered that I had finished with being a teenager, although technically I still had a couple of years to go. I was now Jimmy Green – no longer John or Johnny (I didn't like being called Johnny as it had another meaning). Jimmy suited me fine.

Later it transpired that I was the oldest, and shortest (just managing to scrape over the five foot two inch mark) of the group of the 62nd entry of RAF Apprentice that went to Cranwell. It was designated as the 2M6 entry. The '2' signified that we would complete our training and 'pass out' in 1952 and the '6' indicated that it would be in the June of that year. (Later I believe that it was to become the 2M5 entry when the passing-out date was brought forward).

At Hornchurch we had each been given travel warrants (tickets) for the train journeys from our homes to the railway station at Wendover.

As new entrants were travelling from all parts of the UK, not everyone turned up at Wendover at the same time. Lorries were sent to collect batches of recruits from the trains as they arrived. We were met, gathered up and piled into a lorries, and transported the short distance to RAF Halton Apprentice School.

When we reached Halton and disembarked, we were assembled to march (I use that term in a very loose sense as we had yet to be introduced to the niceties of the parade ground) to a barrack-room. As we were 'marched' past the barracks, or 'flights', quite a few of the 'old hand' apprentices were leaning out of the windows, calling out '*You'll be sorry.*' Once we had been deposited at what was to be our temporary barracks and had chosen a bed, we were told to 'fall in' outside. We were a very varied group, bound for different RAF Apprentice Schools. Some would be staying at Halton for all of their training, while the rest of us would eventually be despatched to other RAF bases, depending upon the trade for which we were to be trained.

Not only were we a disparate bunch, to say that we were shambolic only goes halfway to describing us as we made our way to the stores to be 'kitted out'. At a long counter we stepped forward, three or four at a time, to be issued with our uniforms and other items by a small army of RAF storemen, who bombarded us with items of uniform together with a litany of phrases such as '*underpants cellular three, airman for the use of*'', as they thrust the items across the counter at us bewildered recipients. We were all kept very busy trying to assemble the assortment of items into manageable bundles so that we could carry them. Perhaps the most humorous item issued that afternoon was '*housemaid one, airman for the use of*', which turned out to be what could best be described as a sewing kit. Then we made our way back to the temporary barracks, where we were told to quickly get changed into our uniforms and fall in outside. Being vertically challenged, I thought that my trousers were never going to fit me, and on reflection they never did.

As soon as we had lined up we were told to go back into the 'flight' and change into our PT kit and then fall in outside 'double quick'. Again, as soon as we had 'fallen in' we were told (or to be more accurate because the tone had changed) we were 'ordered' to go back and change into our uniforms, and this time to be quick about it. '*Move!*' This was our first introduction to service discipline.

The next few days were a bit of a blur as we became accustomed to our new uniforms, communal living routines and procedures, and the basics of drill. Unfortunately on the second day I, together with several others, had to report to see the Medical Officer (MO); that is, we went 'on sick parade'. Although as a youngster I had been able to run across stony shingle barefoot without any trouble, it had not prepared me for the hazards of new RAF boots and 'socks airman for the use of'. I had acquired serious blisters on both of my heels. I was suitably plastered up and declared fit to resume drill training in the afternoon. My heels remained quite painful for two more days, but strangely enough I quite enjoyed the 'square-bashing', although I am sure that this could not have been the case for one of the new entrants, who somehow had incurred the wrath of the NCO who was putting us through our paces. With a rifle held above his head in both hands, the unfortunate entrant was ordered to double round the parade ground, while the NCO shouted commands at him: '*Get those knees up*', '*look up*', '*I didn't tell you to stop*', and one comment that has stuck with me ever since, and was in the true style of film depictions of sergeants majors that were to follow some time later: '*I'll break your mother's heart before you break mine!*'

Just over a week later, those of us who were to be trained elsewhere were transported by lorry and train to our new destinations. As I disembarked from the lorry I was aware that I had arrived at Cranwell, and although it was just down the road from the college that had been my original target when I had first applied to become an officer cadet, as far as I was concerned, it was a million miles away.

My first impression of the barracks at Cranwell was that they were a vast improvement on those at Halton; they had a 'friendlier face'. Inside they were lighter, brighter and cleaner – much cleaner. Things were looking up. Shortly after we arrived the group had been divided into two parts, and about a dozen of us were shown into one of the occupied Flights, but its residents were not 'at home' – they would have been elsewhere on the camp involved with their training. The Flight was clean with a sparkling shiny floor and everything was extremely ordered. As we made our way in we were told to use the floor pads. These were torn-up pieces of blanket folded into pads of several layers. We shuffled across the shiny floor as if we were ice-skating and it then became clear why the floor was in such a pristine state.

There were about two dozen beds in the Flight, arranged along both sides, and two beds at the opposite end to the entrance door. The Leading Apprentice who was showing us round had one stripe on his arm to signify his rank, and he was to be one of the two Leading Apprentices who would be in charge of our Flight. He told us to gather round the first bed on the right-hand side. Looking around, it could have been any of the beds, because they all had identical arrangements. At the foot of the bed was a wooden grey trunk. The mattress was folded in three, and placed at the head of the bed, with the bedding neatly folded, with a folded blanket keeping it all together in a box shape, and it was set on top of the mattress. Alongside the bed there was a wooden open-fronted two-shelved locker with a mug and cutlery arranged on the top of it, together with other items neatly arranged on the two shelves. Mounted on the wall above the bed there was a metal locker which was about three feet wide and two feet high and two feet deep. The two doors of the locker were opened at precisely ninety degrees to the wall. In the wall locker, we were told, was where the clothes such as shirts, vests and pants etc had to be placed (for display). There appeared to be piles of small rectangular boxes of white and air-force blue stacked in small neat piles on the shelves in the metal wall locker. There is always one in a crowd that asks the daft question. OK, it was me. '*Where do we get those boxes to put the clothes in?*' The withering look told me that I had seriously erred, and the tone of the reply confirmed it: '*Those are not boxes – they* **are** *the underpants, vests and shirts. You make cardboard formers and fold your clothes carefully. And you address me as 'Leading Apprentice' when you speak to me.*' He paused and then added: '*Are there any more stupid questions?*' Where do we get the cardboard didn't seem to be the question to ask at that time, so I didn't.

Eventually we were taken to the barrack room that was to be our home and Flight for the next three years. We were Flight B in Squadron B. We were informed that there were three squadrons, and each was situated in its own two-storey H block. Members of a squadron were identified by the colours of the chequers on their hatband. Ours were green and black.

We were soon to discover how and why the Flight was so clean neat and tidy. By today's standards, the way the lockers and beds were laid out and lined up would indicate that whoever set up this system was seriously suffering from an Obsessive Compulsive Disorder, but that was the standard which we would have to live by for the next three years.

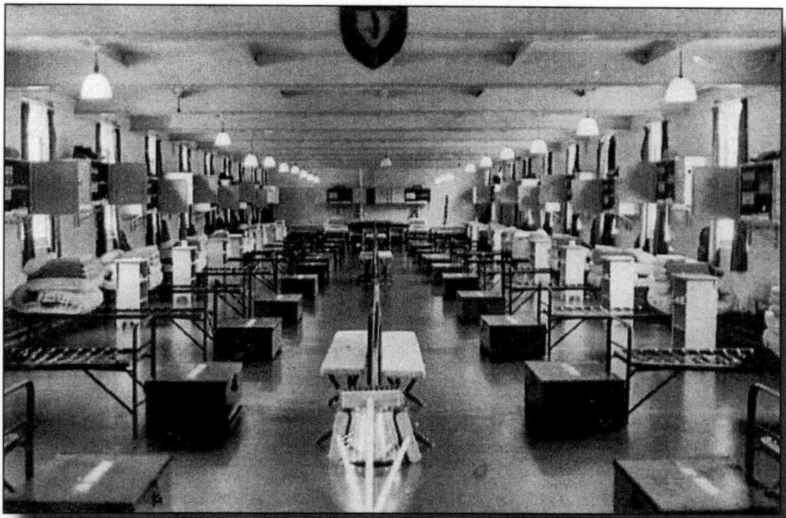

A typical Flight. Photograph taken by Brian Tichener 65th (3M5) Entry

It turned out that Friday night was dedicated to cleaning, or 'bull night' as it was known, and this how it proceeded. The first task was to clean the Flight, and that started with the floor. All the wooden trunks and wooden lockers with contents were placed on the beds. The beds on one half of the Flight were carried, not pushed, to the other side, so that all of the beds were on one side. One of the two leading apprentices, whose beds were at the end of the Flight furthest from the entrance, using a spatula-like tool, splatted dollops of floor polish on the floor from a large tin. We were instructed to form a line along part of the length of the newly created space, and to place our hands on the waist of the apprentice in front of us, just as if we were about to do the conga. Instead of a dance, we were set to shuffling, from side to side and in step, at intervals gradually moving down the Flight so that the whole length became polished. It seemed to go on forever but in reality it was only for about half an hour. Then, not daring to venture off the floor pads, we carefully moved all the beds onto the now polished half of the Flight, and repeated the process for the other half.

Once the floor had been buffed up and the beds were back in place, it was time to clean up our own bed spaces. This involved carefully dusting the metal locker inside and out, first having removed the display contents, that is the clothing, now mounted on formers, to make them look like little boxes (not to be used for wearing). This was followed by the dusting of the heating pipes behind the beds, and the nearest window-sills; next it was the bed frames. Every nook and cranny had to be dusted. With this all done we turned to our personal kit cleaning. Throughout most of the first year, trousers and jackets were ironed nearly every day so this would also be done on 'bull nights'. The same applied to the polishing of buttons and cap badges and – most important of all – the polishing of boots, which were polished every day. The method used to produce an acceptable shine was the time-honoured one in which you gently rubbed a little polish into a small area of the boot using a duster and an index finger in small circular movements and then spat on to the area being polished while continuing with the small circular movements. The process had to be repeated for small areas at a time until the toe and heel of each boot was completed. Initially this was very slow, but after a few weeks it would take less time as the boots built up a nice shiny surface.

As soon as kit cleaning had been completed, it would be time to set the Flight ready for inspection, which in the beginning was every Friday night. Inspection was conducted by the two Leading Apprentices of the Flight, and I am sorry to say that they took their authority very seriously. Once our blankets, sheets and mattresses were folded to form a rigid box shape, the lining-up began. On each side of the Flight, the apprentices whose beds were nearest the entrance and those whose beds were furthest, after making sure that their own beds were the correct distance from the wall, held each end of a long piece of string against the end of their bed frames, pulled the string taut, and then each bed in turn was moved to line up exactly with the string. Great care had to be taken not to mark the floor. The process was then repeated for the mattresses, 'blanket boxes', wooden locker and trunks. Finally the benches and tables were lined up and then before you knew it. – joy of joys! – it was time for inspection. '*Stand by your beds!*'

Maybe it was because the Leading Apprentices had been through a similar process, and thought that they were carrying on a tradition. Or possibly their promotions had gone to their heads. Whatever the reason, these inspections were a far from pleasant experience. We would stand at attention for a long time, listening to the very slowly approaching tirade of abuse, with comments such as: 'w*here did you grow up?.... In a pig sty? ... Look at that filth.*' This would have been when the one carrying out the inspection had run his finger along some obscure part of the bed frame and found a minute area of dust. One particular evening the inspection had gone on longer than usual – it was approaching two hours – and there were only a couple of dozen of us in the Flight, when one of those who had already been inspected collapsed. That inspection ended there and then. After that, inspections never lasted more than an hour unless it was one that was carried out just before a Wing Commander's inspection.

Starting as a disorderly rabble, it was surprising how quickly we came to being a unit on the parade ground. There was a certain satisfaction in carrying out drill routines in a way that we performed each part in complete synchronism. '*Atten...shun!*' followed by '*Smack*' as one sound. This was the beginning of a 'camaraderie', in which the unit became much bigger and more important than its individual parts. Loyalty to the Flight became all-important. I would not like to pretend that it represented the establishment of lifelong friendships. Many members of the Flight, including me, still had their own aims and interests at heart. However, there was this all-embracing and profound sense of being a unit.

Of course, the drill was only a small part of our training. We had lectures in a series of wooden huts and we would be marched from one hut to the next after each lecture. Over the course of a year we were tutored in a large range of subjects including electrical and electronic theory, blueprint drawing, and numerous others, in what was possibly the best education in the country. In addition to the square bashing I enjoyed the educational part immensely and did rather well, satisfying my urge to be up there with the best, possibly at times being the best. We also had time in the workshops where the ultimate aim was for each of us to produce a radio receiver. It started out with us having to file a piece of cylindrical brass rod into a rectangular block with a perfectly square cross-section. I can't say I shone at this task, but I eventually got there. Hanging in the workshops there were large notices with messages such as 'Near enough is no measurement' and 'Care and caution are essential when you work at high potential'.

Outside B Squadron -
Note the trousers don't fit

After six weeks we were given fourteen days' leave and issued with travel warrants to get home and back. An encounter with a naval officer just after I had arrived at Portsmouth was a little confusing and embarrassing. As I passed this particular officer I saluted, longest way up, shortest way down, I hadn't gone more than half a dozen paces when he called out '*Hey you laddie, come here!*' I turned round and walked briskly back to the officer '*Sir?*' '*If I had to salute every serviceman that I passed along here I would never put my bloody arm down, do you understand?*' '*Yes Sir!*' I replied. Almost forgetting myself, my arm twitched, but I managed not to salute him. He turned and made his way back to HMS Vernon, and I carried on to the Gosport ferry. I had the distinct feeling that if I hadn't saluted him he would still have called me back. Later in the year when I was back at Cranwell, I witnessed an opposite kind of incident. We were on a break between lectures when a group of apprentices from one of the senior entries walked past a new Pilot Officer. He was so new that the single thin stripe on his sleeve shone with an iridescent blue. '*Hey! You lot come here!*' They turned and strolled back. '*Why didn't you salute me?*' he demanded. '*We're on NAAFI break Sir.*' '*Oh right*' said the newly qualified, and mystified. '*Right – carry on.*' They strolled on, smiling to themselves.

20

A 'ROCKY' START

It was during my first leave that I met Jean Burtoo. With Brian and a couple of other lads, I was sitting on the beach near to where the old derelict building had once stood. We had been watching a replica Viking ship, like the one that is portrayed on the Gosport crest. It had been rowed from Gosport to the skeletal remains of the pier. Jean was with a girl friend and they were out for an afternoon stroll along the cliffs. They had stopped just above where we were on the beach. I guess she must have liked the look of me because she flipped a tiny pebble at me to attract my attention. The family joke is that I still have the scar from the 'rock that she threw'. We started chatting; I was definitely attracted to her. At the time, she was working and living-in at a Dr Lyttle's in Southsea, and this was her half day. Being in service at that time, especially when you 'lived- in', meant that your employer practically owned your life. After we had been talking for a while, she said that it was time for her to get back to where she worked, so I walked her to the Inn by the Sea bus-stop. When we got there she decided to phone Dr Lyttle's wife from the public phone booth. '*I'll see if I can stay for a couple more hours,*' said Jean as she went into the phone booth When she came out, her face told the me that the answer had been no, and she made a very un-ladylike comment that confirmed this. Nevertheless before she got on the bus we made arrangements to meet again, which we managed to do briefly before I returned to Cranwell the following week. We exchanged addresses and she said that she would write to me and she was as good as her word – she wrote to me every week, although I must confess that I did not reply as frequently. Well, that is how it all started.

It was really special to get those letters, particularly during the next three months until my next leave, and then over the next two years or so, despite the occasional ribbing by whichever Leading Apprentice gave out the mail. All apprentices who received letters from their girlfriends were subjected to ribald comments, when the mail distributor took long, lingering, appreciative sniffs of some of the letters that they were distributing. It was customary, at that time, for young ladies, when writing to their sweethearts, to put a little scent in their letters, as Jean did. Although those of us who received such letters would feign embarrassment, I think with hindsight we were quite pleased because it gave us little of what is sometimes nowadays referred to as 'street cred'. Jean and I met up again on my next leave at Christmas.

After the return from our first leave, we were issued with rifles and bayonets, and this added a whole new dimension to our drill practice. The rifles were old Lee Enfield 303s. Even if I had saved the 303 bullets that I had acquired on my marauding visits to Browndown ranges a few years earlier, they would have been of no use because the firing pins had been filed off the rifles. The rifles were basically for drill purposes, although later we did use them for bayonet charge exercises. The bayonets were the large eighteen-inch variety, which were still in use at that time. We were drilled in the various rifle moves including slope arms and, my favourite, present arms. It was, for me, deeply satisfying to hear the totally synchronised slap of hands on the rifle straps against the rifles, in unison with the boots of the right feet hitting the parade ground as one. The most difficult exercise was 'fix bayonets' which had to be completed while looking directly to the front, and most certainly not looking at where the bayonet was being fixed. There was the occasional clatter of a bayonet falling on the parade ground during drill sessions.

Perhaps it was a case of nerves on the big day, but on one major parade it did happen to one unfortunate apprentice next-but-one to me in the squad. The bayonet had not secured properly, and as we came to attention it fell to the ground with what seemed to be an inordinately loud clatter. The 'unfortunate' kept his head and didn't try to retrieve it. We were under strict instructions that, if we did drop our bayonet, we had to leave it where it fell. *'You do NOT bend down to pick it up!* 'This order was followed by a description of what the NCO would do to anyone who attempted to reclaim a dropped bayonet; it was a descriptive and lurid account of where and how he would put the bayonet.

That particular parade also had another spectacular mishap. It was a very warm day, and the band on parade was playing immediately in front of the squad that I was part of. A red-haired, kilted apprentice in the section of the band that was playing the bagpipes, was overcome by the heat and slowly collapsed into a crumpled heap on the parade ground. The bagpipes accompanied his slow descent with a discordant dying lament. I am not sure whether this was a contingency plan or not, but three of the drill NCOs marched on to the parade ground, picked up the apprentice and the now-dead bagpipes and carried them off 'in step' to the shade of the trees that lined the west end of the parade ground.

Apart from being an implement, 'airmen for the use of', on parade grounds, the rifle also had to be used with the bayonet fixed for exercises, in which we had to charge at and attack straw-filled dummies. Some of the dummies were suspended in frames and others were placed flat on the ground. Throughout the charging and 'sticking', we were told to shout and scream, and use any obscenities that we wished. On that day I was surprised at the extended vocabulary of some of my compatriots.

Whenever I was on leave, it was good to see that the Tower cinema, dancehall and bars were as popular as ever, and of course as I was now old enough to go into the bars in the Tower, I was a regular patron when I was on leave. It was in one of the bars in the Tower, soon after I joined the RAF that I met and became friends with Ken, who was a couple of years older than me. He lived in Gosport Road, and we both belonged to the 'Shorthouse' clan. Ken was a printer in the Merchant Navy, and worked for the Union Castle shipping company.

We became regular drinking buddies when we were both home at the same time. He was on a regular run from Southampton to South Africa, which meant that he had a week off every six weeks. The Union Castle ships would leave every Thursday evening and sail down the Solent past Lee just after five o'clock, as regular as clockwork.

There was a period towards the end of my first year at Cranwell when Jean and I went through a rough patch in our relationship and we had fallen out, probably because I had failed to reply to far too many of her letters. It was so bad that, although I was on leave, I hadn't even been in touch with her. One evening I was out having a few drinks with Ken and I told him that Jean and I were no longer seeing each other. Maybe I was getting a bit maudlin. The upshot was that I suggested that he might like to take her out because she was good company, and she was probably feeling a bit down because we had broken up. About a week later he did get in touch with Jean and took her to the cinema a couple of times, but Jean subsequently told me that they had got on well as friends but that there was no romantic spark.

It must have been a couple of months later, when I was probably feeling sorry for myself and rather lonely, that I wrote to Jean and she wrote back. As a consequence we made up and started to exchange letters more frequently. On my next leave, in addition to taking Jean out, we took Ken out with us too on a couple of occasions. It was to be another five or six years before I was to introduce Ken to Sheila, a young lady who I knew from where I worked. After that we went out as a foursome, and not long after that, Sheila and Ken got married.

In the 40s, 50s and 60s pubs were very male-orientated; not only did licensed establishments not allow children on the premises for fear of losing their licence, but ladies unaccompanied by a male were usually not welcome. There were unconfirmed stories that landlords did not allow unaccompanied ladies, except the Sally Army, into their establishments in case the wives of their valued clientele got to hear of it, and then suspected that the husbands were spending their money on something other than beer. Of course ladies were allowed to work behind the bar: in the 60s one of the barmaids, who I knew very well by sight, from the downstairs Tower bar, was murdered outside the San Diego Road Post Office in Gosport.

The second time that we went out as a threesome, Jean, Ken and I had been to Martha's Bar in Commercial Road, Portsmouth. Although Jean had not had a lot to drink, she had mixed her drinks, and became a little too merry. Therefore we decided that it would be better to walk back to Southsea rather than taking a bus, to give Jean a chance to sober up. With me on one arm and Ken on the other, she was walking along Commercial Road, singing and trying to dance. A passer-by said in a conspiratorial voice: '*Better watch it mate, there's a copper just down the road.*' We had great difficulty in keeping her quiet but managed to get past the policeman without incident. Nowadays, of course, Jean's joyful singing and dancing would go totally unnoticed, but in those days that certainly would not have been the case. If a policeman was at all suspicious about anyone's behaviour he would stop them and then ask them to walk in a straight line. If it wasn't done to his satisfaction they could end up at the police station, charged with being drunk in a public place or even with being drunk and disorderly. Having got past the policeman without incident, we walked the mile or so to the park opposite the doctor's house, where the three of us sat on a park bench for about a quarter of an hour while Jean composed herself – that is, after she had cried her eyes out.

As the saying goes, 'the course of true love never runs smooth'. Well it certainly didn't in our case. Only a few months after this episode we had a second 'break up'. Although I can't remember how it came about, I thought that I had really cooked my goose this time. It was during my next leave, a few months later, that I went to Southsea one evening to meet up with 'Lord Malvern' – actually it was Dennis Jepp a fellow apprentice from the 2M6 entry. He lived in Malvern Road and somehow he became known by that title among friends. We had a few drinks in the Clarendon, which was his local. Although it was quite early and we had been in the pub for only a couple of hours, we decided to call it a day – there just didn't seem to be much of an atmosphere. It must have been about nine thirty. '*See you on the train next Sunday'* I called out and set off walking towards Handley's Corner to catch a bus to the Gosport ferry.

As I walked down Clarendon Road, I went past where Jean worked. After I had passed the doctor's house and walked a couple of hundred yards further on to where there was a telephone booth, on the spur of the moment I decided to phone Jean, just to hear how she was getting on. If the truth be known, I felt a bit guilty and had some remorse about the way in which we had broken up. Jean answered the phone: the doctor and his wife were obviously out. I noticed that she had answered very quickly. I only just had time to say '*hello ...*' and she promptly replied '*I know where you are, you stay right there!*' She paused and added '*DON'T YOU MOVE!* ' then the line went dead. I did as she said, and probably because I was feeling guilty I did not panic and do a runner. The next thing I saw was Jean coming along the pavement, quite briskly and purposefully, in her slippers. You can tell a lot from body language, and I don't mind telling you that I was more than a little apprehensive. At first I thought that she was going to give me a good dressing down and then possibly a hard slap, but no, she came up to me and said quite coolly '*Just come back with me. I want to have a word with YOU.*' She took me by the arm and walked me unresisting back to the doctor's house. When we got there, she explained that she had been looking out of the window and recognised me by my walk.

After a long chat in which I told her how wrong I had been, and that I was sorry, we made up, she gave me a cuddle and forgave me and we made plans to meet again. A little while after that I left and walked the mile-and-a-half back to the ferry, not bothering to catch a bus – just feeling good.

Although in those days, there was no 'try before you buy' in relationships, I am not trying to suggest that, bearing in mind the natural increase in hormone activity, we spent all of our time polishing our haloes. Nevertheless, we enjoyed each other's company and our thoughts began to turn to us eventually being married, and Jean became known as John Green's girl.

Jean and me Below Bar at Southampton

Our relationship had had on-and-off periods, which were usually my fault. No! To be truthful they were always my fault. I really must have needed my head examining. Anyhow, from then on our relationship was on a firm footing, and we still occasionally reminisce about that time when we 'made up' for good.

The time came round all too quickly for me to make my way back to Cranwell, but when it did, Jean came to see me off at Portsmouth Harbour station. Once back at the Apprentice School, Jean's letters resumed their weekly appearance, and I improved my replying to her letters. At the camp, we soon got back into our routines of drill, lectures, workshops and the like, and life was good. I was enjoying all aspects of the training, perhaps with the exception of some of the 'bull sessions', but it did seem long a long time to my next leave. When at last it did come round, on arriving home it was so irritating – as it had been on every previous occasion – that whenever I met someone that I knew, invariably they would say '*Hello, on leave again, when are you going back?*' This would usually be on the first day of the leave.

Immediately after the Christmas leave, the 64th entry (3M1) arrived at Cranwell. This was the time when some of our entry would be expected to be promoted to be Leading Apprentices to take charge of the Flights of the new arrivals. A list appeared on Standing Orders for some from our Flight to report to the Guard Room on a specified evening. Everyone knew that this would be the occasion when the selected few would be promoted. My name and number were included and I attended together with the others – I was not quietly confident, but quietly hopeful. I had been performing pretty well and was achieving high marks in the subject that we were studying. If I was not the best, I had been very near the top. I had kept my nose clean and my kit always passed inspection without too much trouble. I didn't know but that evening was to be a pivotal point in my career in the RAF. I don't know why, and of course I never will, but the Duty corporal said to me: '*Oh, there's been a mistake – your name shouldn't have been on that list. You can go back to your flight.*' '*Right, Corporal,*' I replied, and made my way back. My embarrassment was short-lived because the others who had been promoted soon came back and were being congratulated by the rest of us.

Although I was very disappointed and a little disheartened, I made up my mind to be among the next group who were to be made up to Leading Apprentice. First of all, I had a go at joining the band as a trumpeter. What we called trumpets were really straight bugles because they didn't have any valves. I am afraid I can't claim to be musical at all, but I did manage to master the few of the notes possible on the so-called trumpet. It was only a few days after I joined the band that it was taken to Skegness to form part of a cavalcade. There was I, marching along with my trumpet to my lips, pretending to be playing. It suddenly occurred to me that the tune they were playing was quite simple, so I thought I would give it a try. Mistake! For a few seconds there was a certain amount of discord in the band, but I got away with it and reverted to pretending for the rest of the march.

As a member of the band (and saying that I really am flattering myself, because I could just about struggle through a couple of the tunes that they played) I was part of the contingent that went to the 1951 Farnborough Air Show. We were 'under canvas', in a field somewhere near Fleet. With limited ablution facilities and, no access to irons to press our uniforms, it was very difficult to produce any semblance of being smart. Nevertheless we, together with a large contingent of other RAF personnel, marched past King George VI. After this march-past, I was told that technically I was now allowed to wear a red flash behind the brass trumpet badge on my arm. However it never came to that, because the bandmaster eventually realised that I was not really an asset to the band, so I had to hand in my trumpet. In reality this seemed only fair because the band was quite good, and to be honest was better without me. My only regret was that I never did get a chance to blow a reveille or a 'Flag down', both of which I had practised and managed to get right. The band was always popular whenever it played at any function in the Astra cinema on the base. On those occasions there was always a chorus of apprentices, including me, who would chant '*Sussex! Sussex! Sussex!*' and we continued until the bandmaster gave in and it was played. Then we would all join in and sing out '*You can tell them all because they know sod all at Sussex by the sea.*' Sometimes there were variations to that chorus. There was always a certain feeling of resentment among us apprentices. We thought that Cranwell College had usurped our anthem. *We* were the Lincolnshire Apprentices, they were cadets.[3]

In addition to joining the band, I decided to become a member of the boxing club to adopt a more prominent presence. Within a few months of joining the RAF we all had to take part in a boxing bout

3 www.en.wikipedia.org/wiki/Sussex_by_the_Sea

within the entry. I did alright in that; I forget which member of the entry I was pitted against, but his heart didn't seem to be in it and I managed to knock him out of the ring onto one of the judge's tables in the second round. When the opportunity arose, joining the boxing club seemed a good idea. I did say that it was to place myself more in the limelight but there may have been a secondary motive because, although those in the boxing club had to do training immediately after reveille at 6.30 in the morning, it meant that they went to late breakfast and avoided morning parade, which was quite a bonus.

Joining the boxing club meant that at one stage I was involved in an inter-entry contest at Cranwell, in which I came up against an apprentice about a year my senior. In the first round I took quite a lot of punishment, and at the end of that round my Second said to me that he had heard my opponent say to his Second, that he was going to give 'that fat-faced little bugger' a good hiding. Whether the more senior entry apprentice in the opposite corner had really said that I will never know, but it had the desired effect, because I became all fired up, threw caution to the wind, and in the second round I held my own. Then in the third round I made a mess of him. Mind you I was covered in blood, a lot of it my own, even on the back of my vest, but I won the bout. This was much to the delight of the members of the 2M6 Entry. As a consequence of this I was chosen to be part of the team to represent Cranwell at the inter Apprentice and Boy Entrant Schools in a tournament at Halton.

When we went down for the competition, because some members of other teams had been changed around, it was decided that I would not fight at 8 stone 7 pounds, which was my normal weight. The trainer said I would have to fight in the 8 stone and under group, and I would have to lose 7 pounds. This was only three days before the bout. I was not allowed to eat and had to train wearing two overcoats, the overcoat of the largest member of our team was put on me over my own overcoat, and I then had to exercise with the rest of the team running around in the gymnasium, doing exercises and skipping. After this I was fed with teaspoons of Andrew's Liver Salts to dry up my blood, at least that's what the trainer said. Much to my surprise I just made the weight, but the officials had to allow me to remove my trunks at the weigh-in. My first bout, and last, was against an apprentice who although only eight stone was nearly 5ft 8in tall. I never got near him; he easily out-pointed me and gave me a pretty good beating – apart from being tall he was quite a good boxer and he went on to win at that weight. No more late breakfasts or missed morning parades for me – or boxing.

At that tournament, one member of the 2M6 entry did very well but, his name, like the names of many of other members of the entry, I have unfortunately long since forgotten. However, I do remember a Phil Clifford, who claimed to have been a minor ballet dancer, and had been in a performance that had starred Margot Fonteyn. I never saw him dance, but I did see another of his talents: he could impersonate the way people walked, so much so that we could always recognise the person that he was impersonating.

21
SCARLET FEVER

Although I had resolved to make myself into a likely candidate for making up to Leading Apprentice, when the time came round with the arrival of the 3M5, once again I wasn't among the chosen few. Another time for reassessing where my future should lie.

There was a saying in the RAF and maybe it still exists: 'If it moves, salute it; if it doesn't, whitewash it'. This was very much the case when preparing for any big inspection. I did once hear of coal being whitewashed, but I never saw that. What I did see was the whitewashing of the kerbstones along the edge of the road by the barracks. I saw it very close up and personal because I was one of those doing it. Saturday morning fatigues meant that we were given cleaning tasks in and around the barracks. It was a bitterly cold morning, and Lincolnshire knows how to be cold. I was unlucky to be one of those who were allocated an outside task. Dressed only in fatigue kit, which was not really warm enough because it was overcoat weather, two of us were given the task of whitewashing the kerbstones. I was given one side of the block, and the other apprentice was assigned to the other side. As I brushed on the whitewash I could see it freezing into patterns. It took me just under an hour to complete the section that I had been given. When I had finished I reported to the Corporal Apprentice who was in charge, and he came and inspected my efforts '*That's OK,*' he said, '*but just hang on a sec while I check the other side.*' He came back a minute later: '*No, the other side is much better. Do your bit again.*' So, with numb fingers I went back to where I had started and began all over again. Fortunately this time it was much quicker, but no warmer, and the other apprentice who was a really 'good sort' and knew how cold the job was came and gave me a hand as soon as the Corporal Apprentice was out of sight. So I was able to report back again after about ten minutes to get a seal of approval, and was then allowed to get back into the warm. It took ages for me to get any feeling back into my fingers.

This proved to be a useful lesson in what to do when on fatigues. Once the job's done disappear and keep out of sight, and that is exactly what three of us did a few weeks later. We hit on the idea of getting off camp to a small roadside café which was isolated in the middle of nowhere, just outside the perimeter fence. I have no idea how we managed to get there, but we did. We'd been sitting in a corner, in hiding mode, for about half an hour having cups of tea when in walked a drill Corporal. He got his cup of tea, sat down, and then he saw us. He, like us, wasn't supposed to be there, certainly not at that time of day. He gave us a look which we interpreted as 'I won't say anything if you don't'. We finished up and left fairly soon after that. There was no come-back so we assumed that we had interpreted his glance at us correctly, but we couldn't use that hidey-hole again.

By now we were beginning to adopt the characteristics of 'old hands', and the Leading Apprentices in our Flight had been replaced by two who seemed to be far less tyrannical, and we worked well with them. A small unauthorised concession that we were allowed to get away with by the L/As was listening to the radio for a while after lights out at 10 o'clock. We were beginning to be quite adept in matters electrical and someone had rigged a switch on the door so that the power was disconnected from the radio if the door was opened. The radio, of course, had valves which took a time to warm-up, and this could take up to half a minute. One night when we were all abed listening to our favourite station AFN (American Forces Network), we heard the approaching staccato click of the boots of the duty corporal (not an apprentice), in the corridor. Although the radio was playing music reasonably quietly, it would have been possible to hear it just outside the door. There was a pause at the door, then the corporal threw the door open ... silence. He stood there for a few moments then turned, went out and shut the door. The clicks then started to move away, the radio came on and although the volume had not been increased it seemed to be much louder than before. Another pause, then an increased pace of clicks and the door was once again thrown open, followed again by silence. The process was repeated once more. As the corporal started to move away for the third time the apprentice nearest the radio, and who owned it, got out of bed and managed to switch it off. The corporal must have heard something because he clicked straight back into our Flight with his studded boots all over our polished floor. '*What are you doing out of bed?*' he demanded in a whisper that we all could hear. '*I've got to go to the toilet, Corporal*' was the quick reply. '*Well be quick about it and get back into bed if you don't want to end up on a fizzer.*' We got away with it, but we did have the radio on a lower volume from then on and it was always switched off when AFN closed down at night with the song 'It's time to say goodnight' by Al Bowlly.[4]

I have mentioned that we were becoming versed in matters electrical, but perhaps that became a little questionable on one Friday evening, when we were preparing for a CO's inspection the next day. Practically everyone was trying to iron their uniform at the same time and the fuses to the Flight kept blowing. Some bright spark (pun intended) decided to put a six-inch nail in place of the fuse. The hard wiring burnt out.

Although we normally kept our socialising within our own entry in the NAAFI, on one occasion during my second year I was talking in a small group with some other apprentices from different entries, and it came up in the conversation that I came from Lee- on-the-Solent and used to swim out to the end of the pier. Whereupon one of those in the group from the 2M1 entry said, '*I know you. Do you remember the time when we climbed hand over hand on that bleeding cable, to get back to the beach?*' '*I couldn't forget that in a hurry,*' I replied. Even though I never got to know his name, and he was in a different squadron from me, he was clearly a Gosport lad.

---

4 www.en.wikipedia.org/wiki/Al_Bowlly

Also during my second year, one Friday evening after Flight cleaning I felt rather ill and walked all the way to the Sick Bay at the other end of the camp. When I got there and saw a Medical Orderly, he looked at me and said '*You're only trying to get off the big parade tomorrow. Go back to your barracks.*' So I walked all the way back. When I eventually got back I felt really groggy, and one of the members of the Flight who had been FTed, from the 2M1 entry – who knew the ropes pretty well and was a bit of a barrack-room lawyer – said to me *'get into your bed'*. I was only too pleased to do it. He then organised an ambulance to be called for and I was carted-off, back to the sick bay, and admitted. There was only one ward on the base, which coincidently happened to be the ward in which I had been born.

The next morning the nursing sister or matron came in to do her rounds. As I lay to attention, as you did, she said '*pull up your pyjama top.*' The whole of my chest and parts we won't mention were covered with a bright red rash of quite large spots. '*You've got Scarlet Fever.*' She turned to one of her staff: '*Isolate this patient.*' From then on things became a bit hazy. I think that I fell into a coma because I didn't know anything for another twenty-four hours. I effectively lost a day of my life. When I came to, I discovered that I was now in a different hospital about twenty miles away, in Nocton Hall, with no recollection of the journey. Eventually three others from my Flight joined me. Scarlet fever in young children was very common and not worth worrying about, but on the other hand, catching it as an adult could be quite serious. The four of us were in isolation, each with our own room. We spent two weeks at Nocton Hall before we were returned Cranwell. On the plus side for this medical incarceration, as soon as we were over the worst of the infection, to help us with our recovery we were given each evening a bottle of Mackeson Stout. The other three 'inmates' didn't like it. Guess who got four bottles each evening! It was quite pleasant, leisurely drinking the 'medicine' and more often than not listening to Teresa Brewer singing 'Put another nickel in, in the Nickelodeon' on the radio as it was the most popular song at that time.[5]

---

5 www.wikipedia.org/wiki/Teresa_Brewer

Apart from missing two weeks of training, another downside of our stay in Nocton Hall was the fact that our uniforms were fumigated, which resulted in them being so permanently creased and crumpled that it was impossible to iron them into any respectable shape. Fortunately, two weeks after we were returned to the fold, we were issued with replacements. The new uniforms presented their own problems. They made us look a bit like new recruits, and my new trousers didn't fit any better. Our old uniforms, after being ironed almost daily for over a year, had lost quite a lot of their original nap, so they had a much smoother surface and ironed up quite crisply and the frequent cleaning of the buttons had made them smoother so that they shone more.

I would like to say that while I was in hospital I had time to think about my future plans, but to be truthful, I had completely forgotten about my previous setbacks. Once I had returned to Cranwell, I began to give it some serious thought. Eventually I came to the conclusion that the RAF and I would have to go our separate ways. I also knew that if I managed to 'work my ticket' (get out of the RAF) too soon I would still have to spend some time to complete my National Service, but if I left it too late and passed out, it would be almost impossible not to serve the full twelve years. There was another alternative. It was possible to 'buy yourself out' as one of the FTd Apprentices in our Flight had done. The problem with this was the fact that the money involved was well beyond the means of my family. Also even if it had been within our means, I didn't think Dad would be prepared to try to 'come up' with the money. I knew that he would be disappointed with me for trying to leave the RAF.

So I decided for my first move that I would start to perform less well in what we were studying. I was up there with the best, which meant that I would have to be subtle in how I went about it. I soon realised that you had to know your stuff pretty well when taking multiple-choice assessments. Putting down wrong answers, but not ones that were blatantly wrong was not easy. Gradually I worked my way down the ranking. The result of this was that I had to start attending extra evening classes with those who were struggling. This really was mind-numbing, having to go over and over topics that I had understood the first time round, but nevertheless I persisted. Then one day my name came up on orders and I was summoned to see the Wing Commander. As I stood to attention in front of him I could see that he was not in a good mood. After a few questions, in the answers to which I tried to imply that I had been happy when it was radios that we were learning about, but I wasn't getting on so well with radar, he came to the point. '*I know what you are up to, Green. Well let me tell you this, I will keep FT'ing you for as long as it takes.*' Then he paused and gave me a long, hard, icy look to show that he meant it. '*I don't want to see you here again. Dismiss!*' Sharp about turn and I was outside the door

I'd been rumbled: I hadn't thought it through properly. I then realised that probably dozens had tried this way before. I hadn't been as clever as I thought I was. Now it was time for plan B. The problem was, I didn't have a plan B.

In June 1951, it was the turn of 2M6 Entry to go to the Summer Camp at Northcoates. The weekend just before the Entry was due to leave, I went with a small group roller-skating at a rink in Sleaford. Once again showing off was to be my downfall, and once again, downfall is an appropriate word. Not content with being able to do reverse-turns, I decided that I would try to do one foot reverse-turns. On the move, swinging right foot forward, then left foot wheels on the rink briskly rotated through 180 degrees, right foot back to the rink, job done. After doing it a couple of times I thought I would show my companions how good I was. Well it went OK up to the brisk 180-degree rotation. After pride cometh, and didn't it cometh! I hit the rink with a good old thump, landing on my outstretched left arm. Oh boy, was it painful. As I sat on the rink I could feel the cold sweat on my forehead. It was only a dislocated elbow, but by the next morning I couldn't straighten my arm so it was sick parade for me. As a consequence of the dislocated elbow I was not able to go to the Summer Camp.

When the rest of the entry left for the Camp, administration didn't know what to do with me. First of all I was made-up to an acting Leading Apprentice, with no duties. I had been attending the Sick Bay for heat treatment on my arm twice a day for a week before the Entry left, and continued to do so for a few days afterwards. Then I was sent on sick leave for a week. Because I could not bend my arm, I could not put on my collar and tie. I had to wear a reversed pullover under my tunic. On the journey home, as I was making my way across London, I was stopped by a couple of Snowdrops (RAF military police who had a white top on their hats), because I was improperly dressed. Rumour had it that they liked to intimidate RAF Apprentices and Boy Entrants: whether that was true or not, I don't know, but it took me a long time to convince them, even with the documentation that I was carrying, that I was going on sick leave and I could not put on a collar and tie. Eventually they allowed me to continue on my journey, after I had missed at least one train.

Whenever on leave I would try to see Jean as often as possible, but this was not as often as I would have liked. When she came to see me at Anglesea Road and it was time to return to where she worked and lived, I would put her on the bus to Gosport so that she could catch the ferry and then another bus or trolleybus on the Portsmouth side. In general there were no bus shelters. It was common practice, for intending bus passengers to take shelter in nearby shop doorways, especially if it was raining. When doing this it was important to keep a good lookout for the bus, because they were only too easy to miss. On the corner of Ryde Place and Portsmouth Road was 'Rebecca's, a ladies hairdresser's, and the bus-stop was immediately in front of it. I have fond memories of this doorway, as it was where I would kiss Jean goodnight just before she caught the bus.

You may think that it was not very chivalrous of me not to take her home, but because the buses and ferries stopped running quite early at night, if I had taken her home it would have meant less time together, as I would have had to leave in time for me to catch the last ferry. Invariably when I visited Jean in Southsea and caught the last ferry, I would have to walk from the ferry on the Gosport side to Anglesea Road. The journey would be in almost total darkness – although there were some gas lights along the way, they were very few and far between. There weren't any from near Western Way in Gosport until I reached York Crescent in Lee-on-the-Solent. The route home on these long treks was rather tortuous: it was from Privett corner, along Gomer Lane, then along the Browndown Road, in front of the Small Arms School to Portsmouth Road, and finally into Wootton Road to eventually reach home. This trek would take about an hour.

After my all-too-brief convalescence leave I was able to put on a collar and tie for the return journey. When I arrived back at Cranwell, a few days before the Entry returned, I removed the Leading Apprentice stripe, because the promotion was only temporary. My resolve to try to part company with the RAF had not diminished, and it was only a few weeks later that fate intervened in a tragic and unpleasant way. Although it gave me a possible route to achieving my aim, I was not happy about using it because the plan seemed to be a bit too callous and uncaring. Nevertheless I decided to try to follow it through.

During one weekend two apprentices in a senior entry committed suicide together, in one of the huts between the Flights of one of the other squadrons. This set alarm bells ringing throughout our part of Cranwell. The military police were all over the place for a short while and it became obvious that those in charge were very concerned that the apprentices may have been pushed a bit too far. Among other things they became anxious about our mental welfare. This is how I came up with an improvised plan B.

One group of the many involved with checking on our states of mind were the chaplains. Within one of the spaces of our H block accommodation was a Club hut that was used by Catholic apprentices. I made a point of keeping a lookout for the RC chaplain, and when I saw him coming I would nip into the hut before he arrived and start tunelessly tinkering on an old piano that was there. When he came in I stood to attention as customary. '*Stand easy,*' he said. '*Let's sit and have a chat.*' I always found it difficult talking to the chaplain because addressing him as Father did not sit easy with me because of the uniform. We sat for a while; he asked me my name and where I came from etc, and then he said '*Are you happy in the air force? Is everything OK? Are you sure that you are all right?*' '*Yes Sir, er Father ..., I think so.*' Throughout the conversation I maintained a monotone level with my answers and avoided putting any enthusiasm in my responses, although I took care not to overdo it. '*Well let's meet here again in a couple of days time, say Wednesday at about this time,*' said the padre. '*Yes Father,*' I replied and stood to attention as he left. Although it sounded like an invitation, it was of course an order. I was early for that meeting, and back on the piano-tinkling routine. This time the conversation ran along similar lines, with one significant difference. Towards the end the chaplain said '*How would you feel about leaving the air force?*' Inside my head it was *YES! YES!* But I said *'I'm not sure about that.*' (That was one for the confessional box). '*Well think about it, John.*' The first name nearly threw me, especially as I had become accustomed to being called Jimmy. The next meeting was about a week later and when we met again his first question was '*have you thought about it?*' '*Yes Father,*' I replied but not too quickly. '*Maybe you are right and maybe I should.*' '*Then I will arrange it for you.*' It was that quick. This turned out to be a very short meeting, and I had managed to maintain the monotone responses throughout.

Within a month, the RAF and I parted company. During that last month, although I knew I was leaving, I still had to continue attending the extra evening classes. On the last of these sessions, we were dealing with the circuit diagram of a piece of equipment that involved over two dozen individual components. Towards the end of the evening the civilian instructor, who didn't know that I was leaving, asked me to go to the blackboard to draw and explain to the class the function of a part which involved three or four of these components. I went up to the board and drew from memory the complete circuit diagram and explained the function of the pieces that he had asked. When I returned to my seat he said to me '*You've been having me on, haven't you?*' '*Yes sir. Sorry,*' I replied and then added '*I'm being discharged tomorrow*.' The pretence was over.

When I had decided to 'work my ticket', I hadn't realised that it was going to be such hard work. I often said afterwards that if I had worked as hard at staying in the RAF as I did in getting out, I would have ended up as an Air Marshal. But now I had made it.

On that last day I learnt more about the geography of the base than I had during the whole of my service there. Before you could leave, you had to be signed-off by every section from Armoury to Uniform stores. It was a most peculiar feeling walking out through the gates for the last time; suddenly I was on my own, an outsider, no longer in the care of a big institution. Although I was pleased to have managed it, there was a slight tinge of regret, because I had enjoyed my time at Cranwell, and I had hoped that it would have turned out better.

22

BACK IN CIVVY-STREET

In October 1951 when I left the RAF, despite what I had said to the commanding officer at Cranwell I really enjoyed radar and wanted to continue working in that field, and I applied for a job in the Portsmouth dockyard. This proved to be quite difficult as it was a case of being a member of the union before you could get a job, and you couldn't join the union if you didn't have a job there.

The only job I could find with any scientific basis was in the Royal Navy Scientific Service, as an Assistant Scientific in the Metallurgical laboratory in the RNARY (Royal Navy Aircraft Repair Yard) Fleetlands. I was accepted and within a month of leaving the RAF, I started work in Fleetlands. As part of my being accepted for the post, it was a condition that, on three evenings a week, I had to attend an Intermediate degree course in Chemistry at the Municipal College.

The work in Fleetlands was different, interesting and varied. I had to do jobs such as preparing samples by mounting them in Bakelite moulds, polishing them and then taking micrographs (microscopic photographs), taking x-rays of metal welds and assisting the senior staff as required (general dogsbody).

On the day of what was to be my first evening class, one of the Assistant Experimental Officers in Fleetlands told me to go to the office at the 'Muni' (he even told me where the office was) and they would give me all of the information if I just asked directions to the Inter Course. Well you would have thought that by now I would have been a bit wiser, but oh no! That evening, when I went to the 'Muni', I went into the main building which was situated just behind the Guildhall. Incidentally it was the same building where I had taken my School Certificate re-sit exams. I had arrived nice and early and went to the office that the AEO had directed me to, and I knocked on the opaque glass sliding window. After a brief wait, a matron-like lady slid back the window *'Yes?'* '*Could you tell me where I go for the Inter Course?*' Well the words were hardly out of my mouth when I realised what I had said and that I had been 'suckered'. I immediately coloured up. The very straight-faced lady said '*What subject?*' '*Chemistry,*' I managed to get out. She gave me directions and I made a quick exit, but I did notice that behind her in the office the younger ladies at their typewriters seemed to find it quite amusing; it was probably a standing joke in the office. When I went into work the next day the AEO, who had given me the direction, said to me '*Did you find the course OK?*' '*Yes,*' I lied. I wasn't going to give them – they were all in on it – the satisfaction of enjoying their send-up.

In fact, the Chemistry course turned out to be an absolute disaster. At school I had taken Physics for my science subject and had no knowledge of chemistry whatsoever. I didn't even know the Periodic Table. I suppose it is part of my psyche, but I was never happy unless I was up there performing with the best, and it did not sit well with me to have to take on the role of the 'dummy' in the class. Even though I was doing my very best, I was struggling. The only redeeming part of being on this course was that Jean would come to meet me after the lectures, when she could get time off from the doctor's, and we would go to Verrecchia's, a coffee and ice-cream parlour in the Guildhall square, for our 'Knickerbocker Glories'. There were romantic cubicles which were very popular with courting couples, including us. I stuck the course for four months but I was lost and decided that metallurgy was not for me.

My lack of knowledge of chemistry manifested itself when I was assisting AEOs and EOs in the laboratory. One day one of them who had been working with some Potassium Cyanide said to me '*would you get rid of this down the drain?*' He handed me a glass dish and I took it outside and poured the contents into a drain. When I got back, the one who had asked me to get rid of the chemicals said '*You put it in the poison drain OK then?*' '*Poison drain?*' I had no idea what or where the poison drain was. When I showed him where I had poured the contents of the glass dish he said, '*You have probably poisoned all the fish in the upper reaches of the harbour – there was enough in that dish to kill everyone in Gosport. Don't tell anyone about this.*' I didn't. That morning I spent a great deal of time washing my hands in the washroom. Fortunately I wasn't a 'Dumbo' in everything I did. Although I was not to blame for the incident with the poison drain, because no-one had told me about it, I did feel guilty. In the next unfortunate occurrence I was completely innocent, and didn't feel guilty at all. One of my duties was to take x-rays of pictures of test welds and fractures in metal components, using an x-ray machine which I was told had been removed from a German U-boat. As this machine was used for x-raying metals, it produced very hard (hazardous) radiations.

At the business-end of the machine there was a rod-like protrusion, I was shown how to focus the apparatus, and how to place a lead shield which had to be moulded over the 'rod'. When I carried out the required x-ray procedures I was instructed how to set the level of the exposure, and how to switch on the timer and delay together with a light on the door, to show that the x-ray machine was in operation. After switching on, I had to go to the opposite end of the hut in which the laboratories were situated.

I had been carrying out these tests for a couple of months when one day, one of the scientists said to me that he wanted to check the radiation pattern, to make sure that it was safe for everyone in the lab. I set up a typical run and he said '*Good, well done, that's exactly right, Jimmy,*' then he took out a Geiger-counter from its box and said '*right let's do a live run while I check the radiation pattern.*' This time, after I had switched on we stayed in the room. The EO who was conducting the test walked round the apparatus with the Geiger-counter. All was going well until near the end of the test – in one small corner near the x-ray machine, the counter went berserk. It transpired that although I had done everything correctly, as I had been told, on every occasion that I had taken any x-ray pictures, I was sending a narrow beam of high intensity hard x-rays straight through the canteen which was about thirty yards from the laboratory. We also kept quiet about that.

One of the tasks that I was delegated to do was to check aluminium aero engine castings in the workshop. Not a job I relished, but it was not difficult or dirty or dangerous. All I had to do was to treat with an acid certain areas near the holes in which the piston sleeves were fitted, and then inspect the area for any sign of porosity. The problem was that the person who was working on a particular block would already have done quite a bit of work on it; by the time I got to do the test, and if the engine block failed, that work counted for nothing, and the block would be returned to the manufacturer. I had to make a note of the engine number and state 'porous' or 'non-porous'. When I came across a porous one, it was always a case of blaming the messenger, because wasted work was lost bonus for whoever was working on that casting, and they always blamed me and questioned my findings. I really hated porous engine blocks. One day there was a very bad batch, and by lunch-time I had had to condemn seven castings. On the last one I was so fed up with the flack that I was receiving that instead of writing 'porous' I wrote 'poor as'. Unfortunately the typist in the typing pool didn't recognise my sarcastic cynicism, and typed 'poor as' into the official report as I had written it. That report, in a bound form, ended up somewhere in the Admiralty in London. A copy came back to the SSO (Senior Scientific Officer) or boss … he was not best pleased.

My career in the Royal Navy Scientific Service was coming to an end anyway, but thankfully not because of that report.

23

MARCONI MAN

I am not sure whether it was stories that Ken had told me about his life on board the Union Castle ships, or the glossy brochure advertising the course in which I was interested, that had an artist's impression on the front cover showing a sandy beach with dusky maidens wearing just hula-hula skirts and happy smiles. Whatever the reason, I saved up enough money to take a Merchant Navy Radio Officer's course, and in the April of 1952 I enrolled and started the course at Southampton University College, which became a University soon after.

After a year I took the PMG (Postmaster General) certificate exam, passed, and in March 1953 joined the Merchant Navy as a Marconi Radio Officer. The Marconi Company had a credit arrangement with Baker's, a uniform outfitters in Southampton which enabled newly qualified personnel joining the company to buy

Showing off my new uniforms

their uniform. Marconi gave us each a list of what we needed, and we were free to go to the outfitters at our leisure. This was a completely different experience to that when I joined the RAF – this time we were carefully measured and the trousers actually fitted. Taking the uniforms home and showing them off to the family and friends made me realise that very soon I really was about to go back out into a much bigger, wider world.

Within a few days of my peacock act, a telegram arrived telling me to report to the air training base at Hamble for a pre-sea course. It lasted two weeks, after which it was back home for what turned out to be a very brief stay. Within 48 hours I received a telegram telling me to join the P&O ship *Corfu* in the King George V docks in London. That day I made my way to the big city. The Union Jack Club near Waterloo, which I had used when I was in the RAF, was not an option because it was only for members of HM armed forces, and the hotel in Waterloo station was full. Consequently I had to spend a night in a shabby back-street hotel near the station. However, the problem that Dad had warned me about didn't occur.

Next morning I presented myself at the ship and went to meet the Chief Radio Officer – I was to be the fourth radio officer. He told me the ship was to be in dock for two weeks, but I could stay on board and make myself comfortable, and make myself familiar with the ship. Then he said to me: '*can you touch type?*' '*No,*' I replied and he passed me a book, a tutor on how to learn to touch type, and said: '*Learn to type before we sail, you've got two weeks. I'm going on leave today and I'll see you the day before departure.*'

For the next fortnight I spent about eight hours a day going through the exercises, over and over again, moving on chapter by chapter to learn the required skill from the book. By the time the Chief returned, I had managed to make a pretty good fist of it. I was really enjoying my life on board. Even though there was only a skeleton crew on the ship, the food was still five-star, added to which I had a very nice cabin on the promenade deck. The day after the Chief Radio Officer returned, I got to meet the other radio officers and some officers from the Purser's office, who were in the same 'cabin block' as me. Before the day was out, some passengers embarked and we set sail for Hong Kong. Our first port of call was to be Southampton, to collect the remainder of the passengers. I was getting reasonably good at typing messages from the Morse-code signals that I received through the headphones, but the euphoria over my newly acquired skill was soon to be shattered. We were sailing down the Solent and I was on watch with the Chief Radio Officer, when a passenger came to the radio room wanting to send a telegram to Australia. I wrote the message down, my first, sat down and set the transmitter to the correct dial setting and started tapping out the appropriate Australian call sign on the Morse key. I knew that I had to get the message off fairly quickly, because once we had arrived at Southampton the transmitter would have to be shut down.

The Chief Radio Officer tapped me on the shoulder. *'What are you doing?'* he said, *'Calling Sydney Sir,'* I replied. *'Well switch the bloody thing on!'* Not a good start.

It didn't take long for the passengers to embark, and almost before I knew it we were sailing down the Solent on our way to Hong Kong. When I had left home to join the *Corfu* in London I had told Jean that I would be back in eight weeks. I wasn't.

RMS Corfu

Although I was sea-sick when we went across the Bay of Biscay (there were no stabilisers on ships, even luxury liners at that time), I quickly recovered from 'wishing that I could die' when the ship turned east as we entered the Mediterranean and the temperature began to rise. Life on board began to be a wonderful experience. Number Tens uniform, which consisted of the white high-neck jacket and white long trousers with white shoes and socks, became de rigueur. Ten days after leaving London we arrived at Port Said where I stepped ashore on to the jetty for about an hour, and I was conned out of half a crown by a gully-gully man who performed incredible sleight-of-hand tricks. I really believed that the half crown had never left my upturned clenched hand, but it had, never to be seen by me again. This was the mysterious East. Then it was on through the Suez Canal where a number of ships travelling through it, in a convoy, towered above the surrounding desert as they slowly and, in a way majestically, made their way south. Someone pointed out to me what they said was the Sweet Water Canal running parallel to the Suez Canal, just after we left Port Said. The water did not look particularly sweet but that did not detract from the magic of the scenes unfolding before me. There were camels being ridden or led on the road that ran alongside the canal together with carts being slowly pulled along by various other animals. In fact everything appeared to be happening at a very slow leisurely pace.

The life of luxury continued on board as we made our way ever south. After we passed Ismailia, we left the Canal for the open sea, the Red Sea. I had not expected the sea to be red, which of course, it wasn't. Neither had I expected it to be a clear, sparkling and azure blue, which it was. Four days later, after we had sailed the length of the Red Sea, we arrived at Aden in the early morning – and we left again in the evening. When we left Aden we were now in the Indian Ocean. Our course was east to our next destination, Bombay. It was during this part of the voyage that I received a reprimand from the Chief Radio Officer. He gave me instructions one morning to go and check the batteries in the lifeboats on the promenade deck, to ensure that they were all fully charged, together with other checks on the lifeboat radios. This meant that I had to undo the tarpaulin that covered each lifeboat in turn, so that I could clamber up a small ladder and lift the tarpaulin in order to scramble into the lifeboat and then crawl around under the tarpaulin, to get to where the batteries and radios were stored. To do the job I changed from my Number Tens into white shorts, a white short-sleeved shirt and white long socks and white shoes, and spent over two hours doing the task. After I had changed back into Number Tens I reported to the Chief. Someone must have said something to him because the first question he asked me was '*Have you been on the promenade deck in shorts?*' '*Yes sir,*' I replied. '*Didn't you know that dress of the day was Number Tens?*' '*Yes sir, but …* ' '*There are no exceptions. Especially on the boat deck which is used by first class passengers. Do not do that in future.*' I made an apology and, suitably abashed, returned to my cabin, as I was not on duty until 4 o'clock, because I was on the dog watch – that is, four to eight in the morning and evening – with the Chief. I got on quite well with him, despite my occasional errors, and I was learning quite a lot from him. Of course, climbing around in a lifeboat in Number Tens would have made the uniform really dirty, but that would have been of no consequence, because there was a first-rate laundry service on board which was free for crew members, and which was very quick, with next-day returns. The items came back in pristine condition and starched. In fact the trousers were starched so thoroughly that it took at least a couple of minutes using a table knife to separate the sides of the trouser legs sufficiently to get your feet into them.

When we duly arrived in Bombay 'The Gateway of India', I had a brief 'run ashore', and it gave me another and different glimpse of the Mystic East. My first impression was a little tainted: I thought that I was following a trail of blood, where someone had been injured, but it turned out to be a trail of betel nut juice. The locals were in the habit of chewing betel nuts and spitting out the blood red juice as they walked along. I was to get different impressions of this city sometime later. After our brief call at Bombay we next headed for Colombo in

Ceylon, and arrived there just three weeks after we had left London. At all the ports of call on this journey out, the *Corfu* departed on the evening of the day that she arrived. After leaving Colombo we rounded the southern tip of Ceylon (Sri Lanka) and headed east again across the Bay of Bengal to the port of Penang. As far as sight-seeing was concerned, the Chief was very good, and always allowed the third radio officer and me to have a run ashore at the brief stops. Not many of the other officers seemed to bother much about going ashore, probably because they had seen it all before. After we left Penang we set sail to the south, bound for Singapore.

It was during this two-day journey that I was to gain a different insight into life aboard. I was, of course, the most junior officer and my cabin was grouped with those of seven other junior officers on the promenade deck. One afternoon, one of these officers from the Purser's department told me that there was to be a clandestine, after midnight, party in our 'accommodation block', to which a few young lady passengers had been invited and who had accepted. He then added that I had been given the privilege of hosting the party in my cabin and the cabin opposite. What this really meant, as I learnt later, was that I was to be the 'mug' who picked up the tab for the drinks.

He then told me what drinks to order and then proceeded to give me a lesson in duplicity. He said to order three bottles of gin, take one of the bottles and soak off the labels, unscrew the cap of the bottle and put it in the fridge. Then when any of the young lady guests say that their Gin Slings or Tom Collins or gin-and-tonics are too strong, that is the 'water' that we kindly use to dilute their drinks. Later that night, or rather in the early hours of the next morning, the party went ahead. I don't know whether the 'fake' water was deployed at any time. In fact I found it extremely difficult to work out what was happening. There was a great deal of 'milling around' – about half a dozen female passengers did attend, and one in particular, a young ballerina who was with some touring company that was heading for Singapore, became the centre of attraction. Initially the lighting was set at a subdued level; after a while it was dimmed even further and the 'party' continued very quietly. It appeared as if the activity had now become dispersed over more cabins. After a couple of hours some, but not all, of the female passengers left for their own cabins. The young ballerina kept disappearing at regular intervals with different officers in turn, for half an hour at a time. Just before half past three, one of my fellow officers came up to me and whispered '*it's your turn after me and I'm next.*' I don't know if it was a send-up or if what I thought was happening was really taking place, but before he had returned with his temporary 'inamorata', I had gone on watch and didn't get to be invited to go where all had been before. This came as a mixture of relief and disappointment. As I saw it, this would be a test of whether I would be accepted into the 'clan'; it seemed a bit like the running jump off the cliffs at Elmore to join Charlie Beeches' gang that I had done all those years ago. As I had a long-time girlfriend at home, I was really uncomfortable about it, and had decided that if and when my turn came, I would take the young lady to my cabin and say that, if she didn't mind, could we just sit and talk – that is, if I could maintain my resolve. In fact I was not sure that she would have suggested any other activity with me, because even without standing on the tips of her toes, as ballerinas do, she was about four or five inches taller than me. Fortunately I was never put to the test. This incident gave me a different perspective of what it meant to be an officer and a gentleman. I know that sounds a bit prudish of me, but I really thought the trick with the gin was a bit underhand. Plying a young lady with drink in order to have your 'wicked way' with her was one thing, but the fake water didn't seem quite on. Years later, when I saw the film *School for Scoundrels*, it occurred to me that the 'substitute' water could easily have been included in the film's collection of 'dirty tricks'.

When we arrived at Singapore, the young ballerina and colleagues plus some other passengers disembarked, and later that day we headed for our final destination – Hong Kong, where we arrived on 3 May. I was quite in awe of this oriental city. We berthed alongside at Kowloon, the mainland part of Hong Kong. After the remaining passengers had disembarked, the unloading and loading of the main part of our cargo began. This was to be a longer stop and there was plenty of time for runs ashore. I took a ferry trip across to Victoria or Hong Kong Island, where I took a trip to the top of the Peak, the highest mountain on the island, by way of the Peak Tram, a funicular railway. For me, this was for me the high point, both metaphorically and physically, of this outward voyage. The views from the peak were spectacular. I took a second trip the next night, and the view was a glimpse of fairyland. As was only eight years after the Second World War, brightly lit cities had not yet become established in UK. After this experience I was very much looking forward to the voyage back home, to tell them about some of my experiences, but fate was about to intervene.

Three days after our arrival in Hong Kong, I was in the cabin of the third radio officer with two other junior officers and we were playing cards. The Chief Radio Officer knocked on the door and came in. '*The radio officer on the Orna has been taken ill with appendicitis and one of you two will have to take his place – sort it out between yourselves,*' he said, nodding at the third and myself. I was quite pleased that he hadn't just selected me because that indicated that I had been doing OK. We decided to cut the cards for it ... lowest card goes. My pleasure at not being selected was short-lived .... I drew the lowest card.

24
SHANGHAIED

Everything then moved at breakneck speed. I gathered together my 'goods and chattels', some in what was known as a merchant navy officer's luggage. That meant they were in brown paper parcels. The next thing, I am standing in the radio room of the *Orna* with the 'Man from Marconi' going through the various pieces of equipment, with a running commentary that was an express course on how to operate them. I was still standing there with a parcel under one arm – the Marconi Man had left – when I heard the anchor being weighed. In a daze I sat down at the receiver, switched on the transmitter and sent the appropriate Q code message to let Hong Kong know that the *Orna* was leaving port, bound for Singapore.

The trip down to Singapore represented a huge learning-curve for me. My cabin was situated immediately next to the radio room, behind the Bridge. One of the first things I had to do in my cabin was to lower the mirror over the sink. My predecessor must have been as tall as I was short, and he must have been reading 'How to Win Friends and Influence People' because there was a label on the mirror that read 'every day I get better and better'. When I read it, I wished that he had got better from his appendicitis before it became necessary for me to take his place. It was two days before I found the ship's radio accounts; they were interspersed in the pages of a magazine that he had been reading and the magazine was in a pile with other magazines.

I gradually got to know some of the other officers when I went to the mess at mealtimes. A few days after joining the *Orna*, I happened to say in the mess, at the table, that I would be home for Christmas. They just laughed. I didn't think they needed to laugh that much. *'More like in two years time!'* they added. It occurred to me that would be the same length of time as National Service. Apparently what had happened to me was a means often employed to 'press gang' radio officers into the British India (BI) fleet – a sister company to P&O. They knew that I would not be going home for two years, and they were correct. I have, since then, referred to this as the time when I was 'Shanghaied' in Hong Kong.

There were just over a dozen British officers; most of the Engineering officers were Scottish, the remainder of the crew consisted of over three dozen Asians, mainly from India or Goa. The *Orna* was a cargo ship with the call sign GJGK; it's funny how some things stick with you.

I wrote a letter to Jean, which was posted off when we arrived in Singapore, to let her know that instead of being back by the beginning of June, that in all probability I wouldn't be home for two years. She told me later that when she received my letter she broke down inconsolably in tears.

Although the *Corfu* had left Hong Kong a couple of days after the *Orna*, she was a faster vessel, she arrived at Singapore soon after us. I decided to go across to 'my old ship' firstly to sort out my drinks bill and then to say cheerio to the officers that I had got to know. I was told that at the same time that I was on board, the ballerina's father was also visiting. There was palpable panic in the air, and there appeared to be remarkably few officers in the cabins on the boat deck or in the public areas. As it was, it turned out that the father had come on board to thank the officers for looking after his daughter .... Little did he know! It began to look as if what had been said to me at the clandestine party was not a send-up after all.

After saying goodbye to the few former fellow officers that I could find, I made my way back to the *Orna*. It was then that I realised that all of those I had sailed with, and those that I was to sail with in future, would just be 'shipmates that pass in the night.'

I was quite pleased to discover that the *Orna* was not too bad at all. In fact she was on a coveted regular run from the Persian Gulf to Japan. Although not as luxurious as the *Corfu*, the food was quite good – no more 'filet mignon', but roast beef from now on. My cabin was probably as good as the one I had had on the *Corfu*, but the radio equipment was nowhere near as good: there was no High Frequency transmitter to make long-range connections. Suddenly my world had shrunk and all communications would now be via the nearest Medium Wave radio stations, in the area of wherever the ship happened to be. There was no typewriter in the radio room, so everything was to be hand-written from now on. I was really disappointed about that.

We left Singapore and made our way to Colombo, then up to Bombay. One of the perks of being a radio officer was that once the ship was in port, a lot of the time was your own – there were no watches to keep. During our stay in Bombay one of the deck officers took me to Breach Candy Club on a couple of occasions. This was an exclusive club with a great swimming pool and an exclusive atmosphere. I was surprised that this club did not allow Indian nationals to be members. This seemed to be a throwback to the British Raj which had ended in 1947. It was here that I was introduced to a club sandwich, and on one visit, I also saw a Black or Shite Hawk as they were known, suddenly drop like a stone from out of what appeared to be a clear blue sky and take the meat from the plate of someone who was sitting at a table eating their lunch. Iced tea was a very popular drink at Breach Candy; it was very different and amusing to hear a mother say to her son: '*drink up your tea, Michael, before it gets warm.*'

After Bombay we made our way up to Karachi, which seemed to be a dry, arid and dusty place with camels everywhere. Although we spent nearly two weeks there, I didn't bother to go ashore. Once we had loaded our cargo, we set off for Colombo, calling briefly en route at the port of Tuticorin near the southern tip of India. Then we were bound for Japan, with brief stop-offs at Singapore and Hong Kong.

On the run ashore in Hong Kong on the Kowloon side, I came up against the peril that Dad had warned me about. The most hazardous or productive activity, depending upon your intentions, was to stop to look in the brightly lit shop windows. It seemed that within seconds of pausing to look at the goods on show, a young lady would be standing alongside you. They all appeared to wear calf-length high-collar silky dresses with a slit in the side that went from calf to halfway up their thigh – it was known as the Hong Kong split, and was worn almost as a uniform by the ladies of that calling. Invariably these young ladies, who were offering you their 'services', for some unfathomable reason claimed to be exiled White Russian princesses. If these claims had been true, the Russian royal family would have been the most extended royal family in history, and all of them with oriental features. I took heed of Dad's warning, but that was to change.

Five days after leaving Hong Kong we arrived at the port of Nagoya in Japan. It was here, on the evening of our arrival that one of the engineering officers said to me: '*Well Sparky, it's about time you learnt about the young ladies of Japan and the Geisha Girls.*' A group of five or six of us, a mixture of deck and engine room officers, went ashore.

This was to be a night of naughtiness and surprises. The first was when one of my colleagues went up to a policeman and asked for directions to 'available girls'. The policeman didn't bat an eyelid. He didn't give us directions; he took us to the appropriate area. I was to learn that the profession followed by these young women was legal and checked by government officials and doctors. When we got there, the girls were sitting on verandas outside the establishments. They were not true Geisha girls with the chalky white faces, but they were dressed in kimonos and were very demure. No sordid pestering by pimps; everything appeared to be very civilised, cultured and clean. Before we went into the establishment, we had to take off our shoes at the entrance door (a bit like being back home). A deck officer, who had now taken over the role of my mentor in these matters immoral, said to me, just before we went in: '*Don't forget to tell them you are a cherry boy.*' I was a bit overwhelmed by what was going on and the decision about who was to go with who didn't appear to rest with me. The floors were covered with what appeared to be rush mats. We sat in a large room, and at one stage about half a dozen of the girls stood up and performed a dance routine in a circle, imitating the actions of peasant miners, and singing the folk song Tanko Bushi.[6]

---

6 www.en.wikipedia.org/wiki/Tankō_Bushi

Everything proceeded at a leisurely pace, then after a while couples began to drift off to other rooms. When it came to my turn, and I was the last, I was taken to a room scented by burning joss sticks. There was no bed, but a rush mattress on the floor with brightly coloured pillows and covers. Later when I returned to the ship and discovered what cherry boy meant … it was no longer applicable. Sorry, Dad!

After this it was off to Kobe, and then to Yokohama and back to Nagoya a week later. This time we didn't need the policeman to show us the way; a different group of us went to a different establishment, but in the same area. The evening followed the same sedate, civilized procedure. However this time the other room, although it had the burning joss sticks, also had a low bed complete with brightly coloured bed linen. Now I know that you are not going to believe this, but it is true. Just after the young lady and I had got into the bed, there was a tapping on the door. The young lady said something in Japanese and the door slowly slid to one side, and into the room came what I took to be her father, mother and a young sister who looked to be no more than ten years old. One at a time they bowed to me, and in a state of bewilderment I nodded back as an attempted bow, as respectfully as I could while lying in the bed. I can't imagine what my face looked like at that moment: guilty embarrassment would be my best shot. They quietly spoke to the young lady for about a minute, in Japanese of course, and then the bowing ritual was repeated and they left the room. My guess was that they had come into the room to say good night to their daughter and sister and, at the same time, check me out. The event severely dampened my enthusiasm but it soon became rekindled.

After Nagoya, it was off to Osaka. From then on I restricted my trips ashore to the bars. From Osaka we went across the harbour to Kobe where we spent three days loading cargo. It was here I went ashore each evening to the same bar. When I say 'bar' it was more like a small café, in which the customers sat at tables alongside wall-length windows, from where it was possible to watch the world outside go by. Drinks and food were brought to the tables by waitresses, and I got to know one of them quite well. On the evening of the third day, as it was to be our last day in port, I stayed until closing time – it must have been about eleven o'clock. Just as I was about to leave, the waitress that I had got to know came up to me and invited me to join a group of them who were going to the beach. I accepted, but as I had been drinking since early evening, my recollections of the events that were to follow became a bit hazy. It turned out that there were four of the waitresses and a young Japanese chap, who may or may not have been the boyfriend of one of the girls. We all got into a car which had a bench seat at the front; the young man was the driver and two girls sat alongside him. I was in the back with the other two girls. It was a balmy night and we set off for the beach.

All their conversations, of course, were conducted in Japanese. I had bought a Japanese phrase book when I first arrived in Japan and had learnt a few phrases. Unfortunately when I tried to say 'I don't understand Japanese' I realised that I had got it wrong and it came out as 'I understand Japanese' which resulted in a lot of laughing and giggling. I wondered what they had been saying. Although everything was a bit hazy, I am pretty certain that when we had nearly reached our destination, because the driver didn't seem to know the area very well, we had ended up driving along a very wide promenade style pavement alongside the beach. He managed to get back on to the road and we arrived safely. It was a brightly lit, open-fronted beach bar which was still open, and we all sat on the beach in front of the bar. From somewhere food appeared and I was given something to eat that was rolled in what I took to be a pancake, but it wasn't. It was quite savoury though I must admit I have no idea what I ate that night. Then we all went for a swim, in the dark, unencumbered by bathing costumes. When we came out of the water, as I went to put my clothes on, they all beckoned me to follow them. We went to the beach bar, which was still well lit with more than a dozen customers inside. There was a giant open shower, almost in the middle of the room: its base must have been about five feet by five feet, and everyone

– including yours truly – got under the fine spray of fresh water. There was just enough room for us all to get under the shower, but only just. Although the shower had no sides and was in full view of the customers who were sitting drinking, they hardly took any notice of the naked bodies, possibly with the exception of mine because I was the only non-Japanese person in the establishment. After the shower we all got dressed; it was still very warm, so the lack of towels was no problem. Then we all piled back into the car and they took me to the docks, where we all said our 'sayonaras' and I returned to the ship in a somewhat dazed state. A few hours later the ship set sail for our final port in Japan, Moji, which we reached by sailing up the Inland Sea. I said to a deck officer on watch during this short trip that I thought the scenery was really beautiful. After pointing out some feature to me, he said that this was an outstanding trip in April when the cherry trees were in blossom. From Moji, where I didn't go ashore, when we had completed our loading, we started our journey back to India and the Persian Gulf, calling at the usual stops of Hong Kong and Singapore, with an extra stop at Cochin in India before we arrived at Bombay.

25

A ROBINSON CRUSOE MOMENT

Two days after we arrived at Bombay, things were about to change again. It was now 21 September – the autumn equinox – and I had been away from the UK for nearly five months. On reporting to the Marconi office, I was told that I had been transferred to the *Padana*. 'Ours not to reason why': my first thoughts were perhaps she might be going back to the UK. Dream on! The *Padana*'s call sign was HPZN, which indicated that she was not UK registered. She turned out to be a tramp-ship. This meant that she had no fixed route and went wherever a cargo was needed to be collected or delivered. She was one of the Liberty Ships that had been built during World War Two.

SS Padana

Unfortunately the *Padana* had been built for, and used on, the Arctic convoys to Russia, and she was not exactly ideal for sailing round the Indian Ocean. This meant that in a brief four months I had gone from the high life of a luxury liner to a ship that would fit nicely into a Joseph Conrad novel. It was back to the old brown-paper-parcel luggage. My cabin, together with most of the other officers' cabins, was down in the bowels of the ship, and the radio room was just behind the bridge, with similar equipment to the *Orna*. The *Padana* had seen better days; allegedly she had a top speed of eight knots, but that must have been with a following wind and following current. I'm not sure that we ever achieved the dizzy heights of that speed during my time on board. Our destination was Africa, and after eight days of sailing we arrived at Mombasa. What struck me immediately was the perfume of the blossoms on the trees, which could be smelt long before the ship tied up. We were there only briefly before we sailed south, a day's sailing to arrive at Dar es Salaam where we stayed for a couple of days before moving on to Zanzibar, which lived up to its magical-sounding name. We were anchored there for just over a week. One afternoon, during our stay, half a dozen of the ship's officers, including me, went by means of one of the ship's lifeboats to an island that had formerly been a leper colony: its residents had long since gone and it now was a home for several giant tortoises. We were told by a guide, who appeared from nowhere, that that one of the tortoises was nearly two hundred years old. On another day we went to another small nearby island, about a couple of miles from where the ship was anchored. We waded ashore and did a bit of exploring on our Robinson Crusoe patch. After about an hour, when it was decided to return to the ship, we discovered that the lifeboat hadn't been properly secured, and it had drifted about 10 yards out to sea. As I was the strongest swimmer I volunteered to swim out and row the boat back to the shore. The water was beautifully crystal-clear and pleasantly warm. But, when I looked at the water as I was just about to swim out, I noticed that there was a huge shoal of small jellyfish between me and the boat. I had volunteered, so I had to go through with it. Not knowing whether they had a bad sting or not, I adopted a swimming stroke that would never win any prizes for style but it did enable me to me a clear path through the shoal and I got to the boat without getting stung. Then, using an oar, I sculled the boat back to the island – this proved to be more difficult than I had anticipated, but nevertheless I made it, then we rowed back to the ship.

After Zanzibar the ship sailed back to Mombasa, where some of us went ashore, but there was not a great deal to do. There were a few dirt roads and a few shops together with a small bar about five minutes walking distance up a slight hill from where the ship was tied up. It was quite pleasant not to be pestered by locals asking for money, or to be approached by women offering you trips to paradise for a nominal fee.

I'm not sure if it was a copra or sisal crop that was being harvested and loaded aboard from various ports, but for the next three weeks we spent our time shunting about between different locations including Mikandani and Lindi, where the ship actually tied up to a tree.

It was here that I met up with a couple of chaps from the UK who were living in South Africa. Every year they left their families,for seven months at a time, to work in this part of East Africa. They were in charge of the native labour, and they earned enough in seven months to enable them not to have to work for the remaining five months. It also allowed them and their families to live quite luxurious lifestyles.

During the first few days of our stay in Lindi, I spent quite a lot of time chatting with the two 'stevedores' and sharing a fair few beers with them, which I put on my tab. To return my hospitality, they invited me ashore after work one evening, to go to a local whites-only club with them. It was quite an interesting and laid-back club with a huge sawfish blade behind the bar. We sat drinking and chatting, and it got to be quite late, so the two 'stevedores' said I could kip-down on their sofa. Although it was late, we had a meal when we returned to their bungalow, but I declined the salad. As we were entering their place, I noticed a row of ripening tomatoes and one of the men went to one side and peed all over them. The other said: '*he pisses on them every time we get back from the club and he reckons that not only does it water them, it gives them a special taste.*'

The sofa on which I slept was on one side of the living-room against the wall, below a fine cloth mesh-covered opening, rather than a window. In the middle of the night I thought I heard someone coughing outside the bungalow, a few feet from where I was sleeping. In the morning at breakfast I asked them who it was that I had heard coughing in the early hours. '*Oh that would have been a leopard,*' they casually replied. I didn't feel too casual about it, (urban leopards?).

The two stevedores had a rather beaten-up car which they said I could borrow, but unfortunately I couldn't drive. When I say beaten up, I exaggerate not. On the previous evening when we had gone to the club, as we were going down a hill on a dusty dirt road, the driver said '*hold on! There's a bit of a bump, at the bottom.*' I was sitting in the front passenger-seat. The bit of a bump at the bottom turned out to be a foot-deep ditch. I had grabbed hold of the sides of the seat, but my head hit the inside of the car's roof with quite a whack, because although I was still in contact with the seat, it was not attached to the chassis. I went ashore with them on a further two evenings. The beers during the day were on me, and during the evening were on them. Nevertheless I didn't take advantage of the use of their sofa, or go 'leopard listening' again.

On one of the evenings ashore we met up with an Anglo-Indian chap who was allowed to use the club. He worked for an agency that was plotting the location and movement of locust swarms. He had a Land Rover which seemed to be in much better nick than the stevedores' car. It was decided to go, in the Land Rover, to another club a few miles away – it may have been Mikandani. The appearance of the Land Rover was deceptive. It was quite dark, and Africa knows how to be dark when it wishes. Just after we had crossed a narrow elevated dirt track, about four hundred yards long across a swamp, we went up a slight incline in the track. On cresting the top of the incline, in the headlights was a leopard. The 'Locust Locator' braked hard but the brakes were so badly adjusted that the vehicle shot straight off the road. Although there were no seatbelts, no-one was hurt; the driver was able to get us back on to the road without too much difficulty and the Land Rover was only scratched. As we were in the back of beyond, in the dark, surrounded by jungle and with no means of communicating with anyone, it did occur to me that if we'd had to brake on the track across the swamp, it's not certain that any of us would have survived. In the event, it turned out that the other club was not very good and we didn't stay.

Once the cargo was loaded we sailed to Mikandani, and at the beginning of December we went back to Dar es Salaam for two days, before making our way back across the Indian Ocean to Calcutta, calling at Cochin, Quilon, Mangalore and Calicut on the way.

26

CARRYING COALS TO COLOMBO

Calcutta was not one of my favourite places. It certainly was somewhere to go to see abject poverty, and I suspect that it still may be. The Deck officers and Engine-room officers of the *Padana* signed on and signed off with an unending regularity, either because they were transferred to other ships or because their 'two years tours of duty' had just started or ended. It was one of the second mates who had been on the *Padana* for some while who, on one occasion, said to me: '*the river Hoogli is the arsehole of the world and Calcutta is a hundred and four miles up it*.' I think that he could be excused for thinking this because the *Padana* spent the next five months carrying coal between Calcutta and Colombo.

It was here that the Captain, who had recently joined the ship, came up with the most ludicrous uniform idea. He told us that we had to wear a standard uniform top with a collar and tie, number ten trousers, and white shoes and socks. This was in conditions where we were loading coal and where there was coal dust everywhere – and it was hot.

SS Padana *in Calcutta, with me in this odd uniform*

On one day during this loading session we lost some of our electricity supply. The normal means of keeping our cabins cool in the ship's lower decks (bowels) were overhead fans; no fancy air conditioners here. Suddenly we were deprived of this luxury of blowing the hot air around. For a whole day I was stretched out on my cabin sofa in my underpants, all portholes closed and the cabin door shut. Even so, the coal dust had an insidious mind of its own. It still managed to find a way into the closed cabin and slowly but surely deposited a fine grey film of itself on everything including me – especially me. Every two hours I would go to the shower room, thank God the showers were working, rinse off and then return to my cabin and resume my uncomfortable vigil; it was even too hot to read. After six showers, the power was restored, so that the fans could get on with their job of blowing around the hot air, now infested with fine coal dust. On that trip my cabin didn't seem to be free of the dust until we were halfway down the Bay of Bengal.

When we were in Calcutta we tied up alongside the coal depot, where the railway trucks with their contents of coal would be unloaded. This was done by hand and carried in baskets on the heads of men, women and children – some of the children looked to be only about ten years old. At night-time I saw the workers, including the children, lie down on the tracks under the railway trucks to sleep with a sack over them, and a large lump of coal for a pillow. This was after they had worked all day carrying coal in basket on their heads. I saw this with my own eyes and can vouchsafe that it is true, and ever since then it has been a saying of mine that 'you haven't seen poverty until you have seen the poor in Calcutta'.

The monotonous routine of the coal run consisted of six days loading at the coal wharf, six days sailing to Colombo, nine days of unloading, and then six days sailing back to Calcutta. Whenever the ship made its way up or down the river Hoogli, with the pilot on board, there was a fixed radio procedure which applied to all vessels navigating the river. This meant that I had to be on radio watch for the whole of the length of the river. Occasionally this provided some relief from the monotony; sometimes there were interesting events or sights as we made our way along the river. As the radio room was next to the bridge house, I had a bird's eye view of what was happening.

On one of our trips down the river, the early light of dawn was just making its presence felt and there was a slight mist along the rim, where the river shared a border with the surrounding jungle. The silence and calm were broken only by the lazy thumping of the ship's engine. It was so calm that the river looked like a giant mirror. As I was gazing at the river bank, there in the quiet morning mist, I saw, and watched for about half a minute, a tiger slowly make its way along the bank of the river. Then, with no apparent movement, it slowly melted into the jungle background without so much as a backward glance, and disappeared from sight. The noise of our ship had disturbed its early morning prowl.

On another occasion the action was far more dramatic. The pilot was navigating the fully laden *Padana* down the river: at one of the many bends, he gave the command '*ten degrees to port.*' The secunny on the wheel either didn't hear the order correctly, or he just made a mistake, and went to turn ten degrees to starboard. The third mate, who was on watch, hurled himself across the bridge, pushed the secunny off the ship's wheel and corrected the heading. As we were fully laden, and despite the fact that we were moving quite slowly, the ship had considerable momentum and the change of course took what seemed like an age to take effect as the muddy bank loomed nearer and nearer, ready to grasp, embrace and swallow our misdirected ship. In reality it was probably only a minute before the ship slowly began to turn away from the threatened menacing embrace. It was a really close call, but nearly doesn't count.

Just after we had dropped off the pilot on one of our trips to Colombo, when we were about ten miles out into the Bay of Bengal, we passed an unfortunate water-buffalo swimming south (next stop Antarctica). It was on this same run, when we were about halfway to Colombo, that we encountered a huge shoal of porpoises. It seemed to stretch for about half a mile on either side of the ship. The interesting fact was that you could smell them, and they stayed with the ship for about a quarter of an hour. It was quite common – and no doubt still is – to see porpoises or dolphins accompanying ships. Often we saw at least half a dozen or so, swimming in the bow wave of the ship. It was fascinating to see these animals at night when they would shine with a phosphorescent glow, like some loosely attached pale-green parking lights waving about under the water at the bow of the ship.

In Colombo there were no jetties and the *Padana*, like other ships, would anchor in the harbour, to load and off-load our cargo from and into smaller vessels. To get ashore it was necessary to use the services of one of a number of small rowing boats known as 'bumboats'. To summon one these boats during the day, a sequence of flags had to flown from the mast. At night, a sequence of lights was required. When I was about to go ashore with one of the deck officers one evening, because I was already dressed to go and he was still getting ready, he said to me: '*get them to haul up red over white over red lights.*' I went to the bridge and told the duty secunny to put those lights up, which he duly did. Shortly after this a police launch arrived alongside; they came on board and asked what the problem was, pointing to the lights. It turned out that it should have been white over red over white. When I told the deck officer, all he said was '*oops!*' I think it was a genuine mistake, and that he was not just trying to set me up, although it was quite customary to play tricks on one another during the long tedious spells at sea.

It was now the end of May 1954, and this trip turned out to be the last time that the *Padana* did the 'coal run'. Also on this trip, when we were anchored in Colombo, there was a French cargo ship anchored nearby, and it was being used to carry French Legionnaires. They must have been packed on board like cattle or like slaves on a slave ship. I don't know whether it was the cigarettes that they smoked or not, but it had a quite distinctive odour. We later discovered the legionnaires were being repatriated from Indochina, after being defeated by the Viet Minh at the disastrous battle of Dien Bien Phu. When we were ashore in any of the bars where the French Legionnaires were also drinking, the most striking feature about them was that there was not a complete one among them. Each of them, or so it seemed, appeared to be missing either an eye, a hand, an arm, a foot, or a leg.

27

GOING NATIVE

After five months of carting coals to Colombo, we were off to Africa again; this time we were to go first to Lorenzo Marques. I suppose the signs were there that indicated the *Padana* was coming to the end of her useful life, in as much as the voyage took twenty-one days, despite the fact that, for most of the trip, the sea was dead calm. We sailed across the Indian Ocean for days on end: it really was beautiful, especially at night on the first watch (20:00 to midnight). As it was a calm sea and there was effectively no light pollution, the clear black sky with its myriad of points of light and familiar constellations including the Southern Cross, appeared to uninterruptedly and relentlessly rotate about us. Many other things made this trip a memorable one: the phosphorescent streams of star-like points of light, glistening and sparkling in the wake of the ship; the luminescent phosphor sparkling in the ship's bow wave; and the occasional visiting porpoises illuminating the water alongside and in our bow wave. It was a very long voyage and we only had one glimpse of land, when we passed Diego Garcia – it appeared like a series of dots which, as we approached closer, turned out to be a small line of trees in the middle of nowhere. Later, during the Cold War, this little collection of islands was to become a focus of attention when the inhabitants were summarily expelled, and the islands were taken over by America and used as a submarine and air-base. Why anyone would want to live in such a remote place is difficult to understand, but I guess home is home. I would imagine that Diego Garcia must rank very high in the top-ten league of the most undesirable postings in the American armed services.

The euphoria we felt on seeing land soon disappeared as the second part of this voyage got underway. We were getting close to

Madagascar when the Captain was taken ill. It was suspected that he might have appendicitis, so we changed course and eventually anchored off Diego Suarez, the most northerly port in Madagascar. I sent several radio messages to the local shore station there, telling them that we were in urgent need of medical assistance. I even tried using some of my schoolboy French, but all to no avail. They effectively ignored us. Fortunately the skipper told us that he was feeling better and thought he was fit enough for us to continue, so we resumed our journey to Lorenzo Marques.

Our troubles were not yet over. We were just over one day's sailing from our destination when the ship developed a problem in the engine room. The weather was no longer quiet, the sea was no longer calm and the waves were about six feet high. The problem actually was not in the engine room but in the propeller shaft, where the governor on the shaft had failed. Because of this, every time the propeller came out of the water, the ship shook itself in the manner of wet dog emerging from the sea. The whole ship shook and shuddered alarmingly. The engine revs had to be reduced in order to try to stop the shuddering and juddering, to prevent the ship from damaging itself. However, this meant that it became impossible to keep the ship heading into the waves, and this resulted in the ship rolling about all over the place. All of the deck officers had a go at being helmsman; I even had a go at trying to keep the ship facing into the waves, but it was just not possible. In reality if the Indian secunnys who were well experienced at steering the ship couldn't manage it, there was no way any of us could have done it. The ship was in Delagoa Bay, the shores of which were very rocky and it was a bit of a ships' graveyard. The skipper, who was now much improved, decided to send a message to the agents, first to let them know we would be late in arriving and secondly to inform them of our plight.

I am not sure if it was the problem with the engine that had altered the ship's mains supply, but when I switched on the main transmitter it blew up. So I switched over to the auxiliary or standby transmitter … bang! That went out also.

I had been on the ship nine months by now and knew my way around most of the ship's nooks and crannies, except the engine room, and on one of my exploratory investigations I had discovered an old lifeboat transmitter in a storage locker. These transmitters only had a line-of-sight range, which would be about 25 miles. It was here that some of my RAF training came into play. I decided to hook up this lifeboat transmitter to the main aerial and tune it to the ship's aerial, to get a longer range. I proceeded to have a go at 'jury rigging' it. The captain became very interested in what I was doing. Despite his recent medical problem, he ended up sitting cross-legged on the radio-room floor cranking the tiny handle of the little yellow kidney-shaped transmitter which was about the size of a small case, while I tapped out the message on the button that acted as the Morse key. Fortunately I still had a working radio receiver and I was able to get a message to Lorenzo Marques, and to confirm it, at a distance of just over 75 miles.

Later that day, because none of his engine room officers had been able to repair the fault, the Chief Engineer crawled down the propeller drive shaft tunnel, which was a very confined claustrophobic and hot environment: he spent almost twenty-four hours non-stop in there, but he managed to repair the fault.

When he came out, he looked as if he had lost stone in weight, and he said he was starving. It was the middle of the day but the captain said: '*what do you want for breakfast Chief?*' '*A dozen egg omelette Skipper,*' he replied, and that is exactly what he had. The man was a hero.

I had got know the Chief Engineer quite well. Many an evening I would sit chewing the rag with him, because it so happened that when we were in certain time zones, my watches gave me free time that coincided with the Chief Engineer's off-watch time. We would order a case of 24 sodas, and between us we would work through a bottle of whisky, or at the very least the best part of it. Interestingly he had a remarkable talent that I have never seen anyone else perform. On at least half a dozen occasions when I had left, about midnight, he would be sitting in a chair near his open cabin door, asleep in an alcohol-induced slumber, holding a half-filled tumbler of whisky and soda. The next morning, when I passed his cabin to go on watch at eight o'clock, he would still be sitting there asleep, with the half-filled glass still in his hand. I mentioned this to another of the engineering officers at one time, who said the Chief was well known for doing this, and was known as 'the Chief who could hold his drink'. To this day I still remember his favourite saying: '*by and by every day will be just like Sunday and every Sunday just like Christmas Day.*'

The second engineer was also was quite a character. He had a particularly amusing party piece, perhaps not so amusing to cat lovers. He would play the ship's cat. That is, he would dress up in his tartan kilt, put the cat under his arm, and then put the tip of the cat's tail in his mouth. Before the cat could scramble free, he would walk up and down biting on the tail, and the cat would oblige by doing quite a realistic a bagpipe imitation.

Not long after the Chief had fixed the governor, it became possible to increase the engine speed and steer the ship. We had drawn much closer to the shore: the rocks were quite visible, less than three miles away, and we were all pleased to be sailing away from them. When we arrived in Lorenzo Marques the next morning, after the captain had gone ashore to deal with the company's business, all the officers – almost to a man – went ashore. If truth were known, we all had had our doubts about ever reaching port. We took over one of the bars near the harbour and got seriously drunk on onion beer. It may sound disgusting, but it turned out to be not too bad ... after the first few. That day we lived on the free bar snacks and lots of beer, only returning to the ship about midnight.

After three days, during which we unloaded and loaded our cargo and had the transmitters repaired by the local Marconi people, we started again to make our way up the east coast of Africa, with brief two-day stops to pick up cargo at Mozambique, Nacala, Port Amelia, Ibo and finally at Mombasa, before heading back across the Indian ocean and the Arabian sea, to Cochin on the west coast of India and then round the tip of India and Ceylon, up the Bay of Bengal, and once again to Calcutta, where we collected a cargo for Colombo – not coal this time, thank goodness.

When we were in Colombo this time, I was in town near the port when two American ladies came up to me and said: '*Do you speak English?*' '*I should hope so,*' I replied. '*I **am** English.*' They went on to ask me directions and I was able to give them a detailed answer. I had been on a tramp-ship for nearly a year and I suddenly realised that I had started to go native. Gone were the days when I would venture ashore looking like Lieutenant Pinkerton from *Madam Butterfly*. I took stock of my attire: I was dressed in bright yellow shorts which were more like swimming trunks, a blue-and-white floral shirt with locally bought native flip flops, and I was wearing round green-tinted sunglasses with a wire frame, which I had bought in Japan and which looked very oriental: they made me look a bit like Hirohito. Together with what passed for a haircut that had been done on board by an Indian crew member, I suppose it was quite understandable that they were surprised when I said that I was English.

28

ON THE WAY TO MANDALAY

Leaving Colombo, this time we journeyed north-east to Burma, to pastures new. Well, not so much pastures as paddy fields. We were headed for Moulmein to collect a cargo of rice. When we reached Burma we sailed up the river to Moulmein and anchored near the warehouses and small jetty. To get to and from the shore, again it was necessary to call upon the services of the bumboats. We spent almost two weeks loading our cargo, during which time, on one day, I was fortunate enough, through the good offices of the shipping agent, to be taken on a 'personal guided walking-tour' along Pagoda Ridge. We went into all the pagodas; they were very impressive and quite beautiful.

Another impressive feature of the area was the nature of the sunsets. Possibly it was the extensive area of green vegetation, but whatever the reason, at sunset the sky – with a large orange setting sun – took on a tint of apple green. It was quite easy to see how this would be the inspiration for Rudyard Kipling's poem 'Mandalay' which starts –

By the old Moulmein Pagoda, lookin' lazy at the sea,
There's a Burma Girl a-settin and I know she thinks o' me;
For the wind is in the palm-trees and the temple-bells they say:
'Come you back you British soldier come you back to Mandalay!'

Most evenings at sunset the second mate and I would lean over the side of the ship's bridge just watching the sunset, by the old Pagodas and look lazy at the sea.

We did have a little problem in Moulmein when, one night under the cover of darkness, a couple of local 'entrepreneurs' paddled out to the *Padana*. One of them must have climbed up the anchor chain and undone one of the hawsers that were used when we tied up alongside. As we were at anchor, the rope was not in use. The uninvited guest must have passed one end down to his accomplice in the boat, and they were in the process of carefully and quietly pulling the heavy rope off the ship. But not quietly enough, because the deck officer on watch became alerted to what was going on and informed the captain, who instructed the officer of the watch to have an anchor link dropped into their boat. This order was duly carried out, and it resulted in a very large hole in the bottom of their boat which then rapidly sank in what was quite a fast-flowing river. The occupants of what had once been a boat were pulled on board the ship and handed over to the local police. The unexpected outcome of this was that the captain was called to account over the incident and compensation had to be paid to the 'two men in a boat'.

After Moulmein the ship's orders took us to Rangoon, where we anchored out in the harbour. One evening I went ashore on my own, as I occasionally did, and in a bar I happened to meet up with some other merchant navy officers from one of the ships which had berthed alongside. Well I was drinking and chatting, and swapping experiences with three of them, and, a bit like Cinderella, I failed to keep my eye on the clock. The bumboat service stopped at midnight, and that had long since passed. Fortunately the radio officer of this berthed ship said that I could kip on the sofa in his cabin, which I did. Unfortunately during the night I was bitten all over by mosquitoes, and my new-found friend had omitted to tell me that the ship would be sailing at six o'clock in the morning, so I had to be off by five-thirty.

I managed to hire a bumboat just after six o'clock, and made my way back to the ship. In the early morning light, the mist was skirting the edges of the harbour as I had often seen it do on the river Hoogli. As the bumboat approached the *Padana*, I saw about half a dozen of the Indian crew leaning over the rails. I noticed them giving each other knowing looks and there were some comments, in Urdu, passed between them, possibly along the lines of 'dirty little devil', but my night out had been perfectly innocent. There had been no pestering pimps or 'freelance operators' that would have required me to take Dad's advice.

After Rangoon it was back across the Bay of Bengal, round the tip of India and Ceylon and up the Arabian Sea to Bombay for a brief call. It was during this brief call in the evening that I went ashore with the third officer, not to visit any bars but to go to the cinema. I had discovered that the cinemas in the big cities in India were very good, and so were the films. In Calcutta I had previously seen *The Robe* in Cinemascope. This deck officer hadn't been on the ship very long, and he seemed to be rather young and unworldly: initially I thought that he had been recently made up from midshipman, but this was not the case. As we came out of the cinema, we were approached by a young lad of about twelve or thirteen. In some places it was quite common to be pestered by those involved in the trade that Dad had warned me about. '*You like nice clean girl?* ' '*Jow !*' I said, which was the word we used to get rid of any unwanted pesterer. (We had been told it meant 'go away!'). It didn't work for the young pimp. He then continued with a line of the most bizarre sales patter that I had ever heard. '*All same inside, just like Queen Victoria.*' It must have been one of his great-grandfather's fantasies that had produced such a sales patter, and it must have been passed-down through several generations. The youngster could have had no idea how ludicrous and ridiculous his pitch was. The image that most 'Brits' had of Queen Victoria was a stern-looking grandmother figure, with a floor-sweeping voluminous skirt, glowering out from one of the many statues that inhabited all the major towns in the UK.

Nevertheless, despite the ridiculous sales pitch, about which Queen Victoria would have been quite justified in saying '*WE are not amused*', the Third Mate had taken the bait. I tried to dissuade him, but he said that he just wanted to go and have a look, so I accompanied him for moral – or should that be immoral? – support to 'the premises'.

When he saw the goods on sale he still wanted to stay; I certainly did not. Apart from the fact that I didn't have any money, and you don't get those services on tick, I was not at all interested. Perhaps Japan had spoilt me for any escapades of that nature, so I left him there. '*See you on board,*' I said and made my way back to the ship. I was disappointed that the Third Mate had stayed, not because the place where I had left him didn't look too salubrious, but because I didn't have any money for a taxi. I had been depending on him. Consequently I had to walk about a mile and a half back to the port, through what was not the safest of areas.

Early next morning we left Bombay, the Third Mate had arrived back on board safely. The *Padana* now made its way up the Persian Gulf to Bhavnagar in the Gulf of Kutch. When we arrived a day later, it really did look like the back of beyond. It was some way along a narrow inlet, where we tied up to what looked like the only ramshackle berth alongside the jetty. Next to the jetty there were some semi-derelict warehouses and behind these you could see salt pans glaring at you, as they stretched for miles to a small town glistening in the distance. There were no visible signs of vegetation and the scene immediately conjured up the word arid, because that's exactly what it was. Before I shut down the transmitter for our stay in port, I invited the local radio station operator to come on board at the weekend for a drink. As there was only room for one ship, he would have had no difficulty in finding me.

The next morning when I awoke, I couldn't work out what had happened; it was quite dark in my cabin, which was more or less in the bowels of the ship. I went up on deck and the sun was blazing, but instead of being able to see for miles across the salt pans, the tide had dropped by what appeared to be about twenty five feet and, as I gazed out, I was looking at the muddy banks of the inlet. Crawling all over these mud-banks were some large lizard-like amphibians, and on average they looked to be about eighteen inches to two feet long. The ship was now sitting on the muddy bottom of the inlet. Resting on the bottom caused a bit of a problem: every time a toilet was flushed, the water flowing into the toilet pan would be a muddy brown. So for the two weeks that we were tied up in Bhavnagar, we had to avoid flushing the toilets during the periods when the ship was on the bottom.

The local radio operator did turn up and had a few beers onboard with me. He was a young chap, spoke good English and had a wife and young family. He proudly showed me a picture of them. As he was leaving, he invited me back to his home in the town or village, the following Saturday, but unfortunately the *Padana* sailed on the Friday and I didn't get a chance to take him up on that invitation. It was back to Bombay for a brief stopover and then off to Rangoon again.

29

A PLATONIC EPISODE

In Rangoon I went to see its most famous building, the Shwedagon Pagoda where, unlike the pagodas in Moulmein, I was not impressed by the cleanliness. Before you could enter the pagoda you had to remove your footwear, as was customary. Once inside there was a wide set of steps leading up to various terraces. The problem was that pariah dogs were allowed inside, and on the steps they had, not to put too fine a point on it, 'crapped all over the place'. Despite careful and calculated stepping, and all of my youthful training in barefoot doggy do-do dodging, it was impossible not to put your foot in it, which I did at least once.

On what was probably the top terrace there was a large gong, very much like the one used in the introduction of J Arthur Rank Films. I was invited by one of the monks to strike the gong which, I was told, was the making of a prayer. It was too late to ask for guidance not to step in the crap. Nevertheless, I did strike the gong, not with a splendid hammer as used in the film introduction, but with a tatty old piece of timber that looked as if it had escaped from a building site.

Even though the Shwedagon Pagoda was impressive with its gilded 300-foot high pointed dome which was surrounded by a number of smaller gilded pointed domes, all glistening and shining in the sunlight, for me it was nowhere near as beautiful as some of the pagodas that I had visited in Moulmein. Probably it was the presence of the pariah dogs that had influenced my opinion.

The first thing that I did after sightseeing was to make my way 'hot foot' back to the ship and soak my feet in a dilute solution of Dettol. Despite this, I still developed an infection in one foot which took a couple of weeks to clear up.

Being a tramp-ship with no regular run, the ship's itinerary was dictated by whatever trade the agents procured. So as trade would have it, it was once more back to Bombay, where the Third Mate was transferred to another ship. No, not because of what he had got up to ashore in Bombay. Apparently he had already passed the required Second Mate certificate and he took up a post of Second Mate on another of the BI ships. It occurred to me, during this two-week stay in Bombay, how different it was to when I had been here before on the *Orna*. Then the officers were granted temporary membership of the exclusive Breach Candy Club. I never took a taxi there to see if I could get in, because I seriously doubted that the *Padana* would be listed as one of the ships whose crew could be accepted. This time I hardly went ashore, and certainly not at night.

Our cargo commitment took us back to Rangoon again. What I liked about this port was the absence of locals pestering you with offers of anything from dirty postcards to a night of pleasure with a local beauty. I went ashore on the first day and found a small indoor swimming pool which also had table-tennis facilities. As I had time on my hands, I decided to try to have a swim there each morning; only a few people appeared to frequent the pool at that time. On the second day I had just had a swim and was about to leave when I saw a Burmese, or mixed-race, young woman in European dress, about twenty years old, standing near the table-tennis area. On the spur of the moment I said '*would you care for a game?*' and she said '*OK.*' So we had a couple of games, and she was quite good, and beat me on both occasions. Two or three times after that, during the following week, I met her again at the pool where we had a swim and a game of table tennis. It was, much to my surprise and pleasure, a totally platonic episode. On what turned out to be the last time that I saw the young woman, just before I left to return to the ship, she asked me if I would like join her and her sister's family for Christmas dinner. I thanked her and her sister and said that I would be pleased to accept their kind invitation. It was not to be. On Christmas Eve, out of the blue, we sailed for Mauritius – cargo called.

The ship stopped briefly at Colombo to collect some cargo, supplies and fuel before setting out across the Indian Ocean. We arrived at Port Louis on 9 January just nine days after leaving Colombo, which was pretty good going for the *Padana*.

Elevenses on The Padana *in Mauritius*

30

WHAT ARE YOUR INTENTIONS?

I liked Mauritius very much indeed, but was soon to experience a rather unnerving incident. Not long after we arrived, the captain arranged a sun-downer and invited some local dignitaries to the party. Among the guests there was a rather attractive-looking young Creole lady, and at the earliest opportunity I started talking to her. OK, I was chatting her up. My problem was that I had not yet developed sufficient social etiquette skills, so I spent rather too long talking to her and not circulating enough. Eventually I asked her if she would like to have a guided tour of the ship, and she said that she would. Therefore I gave her the grand tour, which included my cabin. When we returned to the party ... well, have you ever been in a situation when suddenly all conversation stops and everyone is looking at you? It was one of those moments. The silence was broken only when someone said '*would you like to show* **me** *round the ship now?*' It was a rhetorical question and it caused a few laughs, especially as it was one of the male guests that said it ... well, I think it was a rhetorical question.

The truth of the matter was that I hadn't done anything. I hadn't even touched her hand. I certainly had not been 'showing her the golden rivet' as the nautical saying goes, although everyone assumed that I had, including the captain who did not look too pleased. Nevertheless, I did arrange to meet the young lady the next day to go swimming. I had heard that there were some very beautiful beaches on the island.

The next day I went ashore with two other officers, the Third Mate and the Third Engineer and we shared a taxi. They were going sightseeing, and it was agreed that I should be dropped off on the way. When we arrived at the young lady's address, I was not particularly impressed with the building and its tin roof, so I said to my companions: '*drive on – I'll come with you two.*' They were enjoying my discomfort too much and said '*No!*' And with that, they shoved me out of the taxi.

There I was, with my towel and bathers tucked under my arm, in a kind of no-man's land. I made my way to the front door and discovered that the house was much better than my first impression. I was met at the door by the young lady, who said she would not be able to go swimming, as it was the wrong time of the month. She then invited me inside and showed me into a room, and asked me to take a seat, indicating what could be best described as a kitchen chair in the middle of the room.

When I had sat down, she called in two people who I guessed were her grandmother and grandfather, I stood up, shook hands with them, and was introduced. (It was indeed the grandparents). Next she asked her mother to come in, again an introduction was made and again I sat down. Finally she asked her father to come in and the introduction process was repeated. Then the 'interrogation' began, but all very pleasantly. How old was I? Where in England did I live? What were my prospects? What kind of salary did I receive? And *could I support a family*? It was a nice hot day, but suddenly the room temperature appeared to drop by several degrees. My only thoughts were 'I never touched her.' Once the interrogation was over, we had tea and cakes. After this I was taken sightseeing in their car, up to the reservoir in the extinct volcano and through the sugar cane fields, then to a local school. It turned out that the young lady was a teacher in the school that we drove past. Her father was a fairly important person; he was in charge of the water supplies for the whole island, which was why we had visited the reservoir. The father drove the car and in the front seat was a man that I took to be the young lady's brother. I was in the back seat with the young lady, with what I believe was another brother who sat between us. From the conversations, I gathered that there were a further two brothers, both in England – one was a university lecturer, and the other was a flying officer in the RAF at Thorney Island. That was a bit close to home!

In the evening after the sightseeing, I was taken to a restaurant in town. Don't forget, I was still dressed for the beach. This time one of the brothers drove the car, the other sat in the front, and I was in the back with the young lady. I don't know we were drinking – probably it was the locally produced white rum, the neat raw stuff, not Bacardi. Whatever it was, it was pretty potent. As I had been on the *Padana* for over a year, sailing here there and everywhere around the Indian Ocean, drinking whisky and gin had been the main way of passing the time at sea. In fact it was customary for me, like all of the officers, to 'get through' several bottles of each a week. Consequently, I was quite used to strong drink. Even though we had only had a few, I soon realised that I was beginning to get a bit inebriated, because on the occasions when they lapsed into speaking Creole French, I was able to follow the gist of what they were talking about from my schoolboy French. Although at school I had been quite good at French reading, writing, and grammar, I had struggled with spoken French. But the local alcohol, with its inhibition-reducing effect, was working its magic.

The evening passed by very pleasantly, but I still had made no physical contact with the young lady. They dropped me at the docks, and we made arrangements to meet the next evening. I deliberately kept it vague, saying something to the effect that I would if I could, but it might not be possible. Then I shook hand with them all … first physical contact, said cheerio, and caught a bumboat back to a safe haven on the ship.

I didn't go ashore again for the rest of the week. I never got to the beach. I don't mind telling you that I was very pleased when we sailed from Mauritius. Don't get me wrong – she was a very attractive young lady, but I would soon be going home to the one that I was in love with and who, for me, was even more attractive.

From Port Louis we made our way to Mozambique, then on to Nacala and Beira. It was at Beira that for the first time since leaving

London on the *Corfu*, I experienced a real feeling of loneliness and isolation. Was I getting homesick? One late afternoon when it was pressing on towards evening, just before sunset, I went for a walk to where I had been informed there was a swimming pool that we were allowed to use. It was a walk of over a mile along a coastal road.

Armed with my bathers and towel, I set off along this dirt-edged road. There was no traffic or pedestrians and as I approached the pool, which was alongside the road with no fencing – in fact it was completely open on all sides – there was just one young female (most likely Portuguese) in the water. When I was about fifty yards from the pool, she got out and walked off towards one of the rather splendid houses on the opposite side of the road facing the sea. After I had had a swim and dried myself, the sun was just about to hide itself behind the horizon and the lights were going on in the houses. There were no street lights on this stretch of road, but it was not difficult for me to find my way back to the ship, because of the light coming from the coastal houses, and the lights in the distance near the port. As I walked back, I could hear the sounds of people sitting down for their evening meal, occasional laughter and music. Suddenly I remembered my own family, and became acutely aware that they were thousands of miles away, and I wondered what they were doing at that moment. I never came across another living soul until I reached the entrance to the port.

In all of the major towns in Mozambique there was a curfew for the Africans who worked in them. By nightfall they were banished to their own townships, leaving the towns to the Portuguese, who lived there. It was not until dawn that they were allowed to return to do all the menial work that enabled the towns to exist.

After leaving Beira, we once more made our way northward along the east coast of Africa, calling at Mtwara which was near Mikandani, and then to Mombasa.

31

OH DEAR! JOHN!

I would like to relate something that had occurred a few years earlier because it is pertinent to what happened next. It concerns the matter of close encounters of the amorous kind. Before joining the Merchant Navy, it must have been the Christmas of 1951: I was at a dance at Lee Tower on my own. I was 'going out' with Jean at the time, but she was not there because she was working. When I say I was at a dance, to be truthful I can't dance – being short has always been my excuse. Anyhow, I was not exactly on my own; I was having drinks with a group of young men and women in the bar while the dance was taking place. Towards the end of the evening there were just three of us left: Roy, Margaret and me. We were not drunk, but well into the 'reduced inhibition' stage. Roy and I flipped a coin to decide who should walk Margaret back to where she worked in Hill Head. Roy won.

This episode was quite important, because if I had won that spin of a coin, my life might have followed a completely different path. Roy told me later that the 'walking home' involved rather more than walking. Perhaps it is the brashness of youth that makes young men keen to talk of their conquests … well, he said that they ended-up on the cliffs tops towards the Hill Head end of Lee. There were no bright street-lights at that time to inhibit them. According to Roy, Margaret was very keen and when they were at the climatic point of their activity, Margaret suddenly exclaimed '*Oooooh Look, the seven sisters!*' She was referring to the constellation of stars, and was obviously looking skywards at the time. It goes without saying that he was not. He never made it clear whether she was disinterested in the proceedings or if it was the equivalent of the modern 'Yes! Yes! Yes!'

Nine months later she became a mother. They never got married. In fact, I am not sure if they ever went out again, and I don't think that she ever named the father.

When I was away in the Merchant Navy, Jean would write to me every week, as she had done when I was in the RAF. I vividly remember a letter that Jean sent me and which I received at Mombasa on 14 February 1955, ironically on St Valentine's day, a month after the 'adventure' in Mauritius. In it she wrote 'Dear John'. That was a shock for a start – not the usual endearments – and the letter lacked the usual smell of perfume. 'I have met a nice chap …' At this point I felt decidedly apprehensive and was ready for the worst. Had my naughty escapades of sowing my wild oats in the land of the Rising Sun resulted in the setting of the Sun on our Relationship? Of course I hadn't mentioned any of my shenanigans in Japan. Anxiously I read on … 'He has asked me if he could take me to the cinema. Would that be alright, just for the company?' What a relief. But that was short-lived as I next read …. 'His name is Roy, and you probably know him'. At least it was not a real 'Dear John' letter.

Normally I was rather slow in answering Jean's letters, with a 'send one off at the next port of call' approach. You would have thought I had learned my lesson when I was in the RAF, but no! This time, however, I wrote back rather promptly …. immediately in fact, suggesting that going to the cinema with Roy might not be such a good idea, in case it unfairly built up his hopes. Mind you, although I didn't know for sure what his hopes were, I had a pretty good idea. I should point out that at the time Jean was working as an usherette at Lee Tower cinema.

It was either in the next letter or the one after it, in which I proposed to Jean. In this anxious letter I mentioned a song that I had heard on the radio: 'You belong to me' by Patsy Cline'.[7] To show that I was serious, I put a signed note inside the letter to the effect that I would pay for the wedding dress: a letter which she could take to a dressmaker. It was a long two weeks' wait for her reply, but I was

7 www.en.wikipedia.org/wiki/You_Belong_to_Me_(1952_song)

so relieved and delighted when I received it and learned that she had accepted my proposal. Not long after this, she went to 'Tudors', a dress shop in the High Street in Lee-on-the-Solent to have her wedding dress made.

Jean outside the Bluebird cafe after my proposal

It was not until years later, after we were married, that I told her about Margaret ... and about Japan. She replied something to the effect that she had been surprised how quickly I had replied to her letter on that occasion. She also said that she had gone to the cinema with Roy two or three times, and he had always bought her a box of chocolates, but he had been a perfect gentleman on every occasion. This prompted me to ask her why she should want to go to the cinema when she worked there. She said that it was just so that she could watch the films through without being interrupted. How disappointing for poor Roy, after investing in all those boxes of chocolate. I don't think I will go into what was said about Japan.

32

TIME TO GO HOME

From Mombasa we set course for India: our first port of call was Quilon but we were only there briefly before moving on to Mangalore, where I received Jean's proposal acceptance letter. Another brief stop, and then we made our way to Cochin, where we anchored off for a week unloading and loading cargo. After that we headed north up the Bay of Bengal, back up the Hoogli to arrive in Calcutta on the 14 March where, to my utter delight, I was signed off the *Padana*. By that time I was the longest-serving officer on board. In eighteen months I had served under six captains and sailed with numerous different deck- and engine-room officers, but now it was my turn to say goodbye to the 'old bucket', with no feelings of regret. I was to be repatriated to the UK. Although I was keen to get home, when the Marconi office offered to fly me home later that week, I said that I would prefer to travel home by sea. This was not based on any love of the sea, but merely a financial consideration. If I arrived home before 5 April, I would have to pay income tax on my earning for the previous two years.

Therefore I was first ensconced in the Seaman's Mission in Calcutta for ten days, after which I was transferred to the *Chinkoa*, sister ship to the *Orna*, as a supernumerary radio officer . The *Chinkoa* would be making her way to London. By now I was really anxious to be on my way, but we didn't leave Calcutta for another three weeks.

Although we only took five days to reach Colombo, we were there for ten days, and it felt as if everything was conspiring against me. I was extremely pleased when, after the ten days were up, we left Colombo and headed for Aden – no Bombay this time. When we were just two days out from Aden, I did something which has to be in the list of the 'top ten most stupid thing that I have done in my life'. Once again, showing off was my downfall, and once again downfall is a most apposite word. When I had been at St John's College, I was a member of the gym club for a number of years. Diving over the box using a springboard, onto large coir mats, was an everyday activity. On the *Chinkoa* I was, no doubt boastfully, telling a group which consisted of a Third and Fourth Mate and a cadet how, because of my gymnastic background, I could dive from a height of five feet onto a solid surface, do a forward roll and get up without hurting myself. 'How oft we mar what's well'. '*I'll show you,*' I said. We went on deck and I looked for somewhere to show off my prowess. I saw a hatch covering that looked reasonably flat and was covered with a tarpaulin, which appeared to be reasonably soft. '*I'll dive onto that,*' I said confidently, pointing to the hatch covering. But I couldn't see anything to dive from. By now a few of the twelve passengers that the ship was carrying had gathered around. I looked at one of the cadets – he was reasonable tall. '*I'll dive off your shoulders,*' I said. That was a big mistake! I clambered onto his shoulders. '*Ready?*' '*Yes.*' Without any further warning, I dived on to the hatch cover. I hadn't allowed for the fact that the cadet would not be braced. As I did the dive, he was pushed back and I lost all of my forward momentum and landed with my arms outstretched, and most importantly, I didn't have enough forward motion to complete a roll. Did that hurt? You bet it did. Perhaps you have seen comedy sketches where someone is hurt and they go into another room before yelling, and you may have thought that people don't do that in real life. They do. I did, as soon as I reach the solitude of my cabin, which was not far away on the same deck. The next day I realised that I had hurt both of my wrists, especially the right one. I had to resort to opening doors with my left hand and to shaving left-handed, which I found very difficult. The ship's doctor said that it would be a good idea to have it checked ashore when we arrived at Aden.

On arrival, the local agent arranged for me to go up to the RAF Hospital, where I had my arms and wrists x-rayed. I was a little anxious because the ship was only on a brief call, and it was scheduled to leave the same day. After the x-rays were taken I was told that the right arm was OK, with just a sprain, but I had chipped the bone on the back of my left arm. They bandaged it and put it in a sling. Now I had to open doors with the arm that was hurting the most. As they were fitting me up with the sling, I looked out of the window which overlooked the harbour. There, to my utter horror, was the *Chinkoa*, my ticket home, sailing out of the port, and already over a mile away. To say that I panicked is a magnitude ten understatement. I had no money and no belongings other than what I stood up in. Fortunately, my fears were unfounded: I had not been abandoned. RAF transport delivered me to the harbour where I was taken out to the *Chinkoa* in the boat that was sent out to collect the pilot.

By the time we had left behind the crystal waters of the Red Sea and completed what was still for me the magical journey through the Suez Canal and arrived at Port Said, my arms were both back to normal, and I could now raise a glass with my right hand without any problem. As a Supernumerary Radio Officer, I didn't really have any watches to do, but I offered to fill-in for the ship's Radio Officer whenever he felt that he would like a break. In fact it only amounted to a few watches during the whole trip. When he was not on watch, I would spend a lot of time with him in his cabin, drinking and chatting. He was a most interesting character. He was about sixty years old, Irish and married to a gynaecologist. He spent most of his time off-duty sitting in his cabin wearing just a towel. Between us we drank every bottle of Guinness on the ship before we reached Genoa where, fortunately, the stores were replenished. One day I noticed that he had three scars on his back so I asked him how he got them. He told me that he had been a captain in the Irish Battalion, at the front, in the First World War, and that he had been shot in the back on three separate occasions by his own men, when he had attempted to lead them over the top. Now I know that Irishmen are supposed to have the gift of the blarney, and I don't know whether what he said was true or not, but from the way that he told of the events, I believed him.

A couple of days after Genoa we called briefly at Marseilles, and then made our way to London, arriving at the Royal Victoria Docks on 30 May 1955. Unbeknown to me, at the time in the UK there was a railway strike in progress. I had sent a telegram home to let the family know what day I was arriving and at which docks. Dad sent me a telegram in reply saying that he would come up to meet me. Because of the train strike, Dad travelled to London by coach, and I met him outside the dock gates as we had arranged. Now it was my turn to take charge. I took his small case and said to him '*just keep talking to me, and act as if you were one of the crew.*' We casually walked through the gates to the ship and up the gangplank. That was how I smuggled him on board.

That night he slept in my bunk and I had the cabin settee. The next morning, I took him to breakfast, and introduced him to the Captain and the other officers. For some reason introducing my Dad to these members of the crew has always given me a feeling of great satisfaction. I was proud of my Dad and pleased to show it, and I am sure that he also appreciated it. After making my farewells to the crew, Dad and I made our way home by coach. I was able to get a ticket without too much trouble. Although I should have reported to the Marconi office in London, being just a supernumerary crew member, I thought that I would be able to get away with it and report at Southampton. Well, I suppose that is not completely true. I believe that I actually I said '*Oh Sod 'em! Let's go home.*'

The next day, when I did report in at the Southampton Marconi office, they were quite niggled, and told me at length that I should have reported-in at London. I was not particularly bothered because they had messed me about in Hong Kong, so as far as I was concerned, it was payback time. Anyhow a week later I resigned, because in just over two weeks after that, I was to be married.

33

WHILE I WAS AWAY

When I arrived home I could see how much had changed in Lee- on-the- Solent, and how people had changed: their lives had ticked on like an orchestra of unstoppable, incessant, inexorable metronomes. They had not remained fixed and set in time, as they had been in my memory. As the saying goes 'change happens'. It took me a little while to catch up with all that had been going on in the two years that I had been away. Most significantly, Jean was living with Mum, Dad and Pat at number 24.

Jean was part of a very large family. She had seven or eight brothers and two sisters, but she – together with a sister and several brothers – had been removed from the parental home because of neglect, and placed in the care of Winchester County Council. She was only four years old when she was put into foster care, and she remained there until she was fifteen, when she left school. From then on, she'd had to fend for herself, which meant she had to get employment that included accommodation. When she became 18, and no longer under the control of the County Council, she had decided to pay a visit to her family, who were then living in Aldershot. The visit was not successful. She said that she felt like a complete outsider.

When I had left for my unexpectedly long trip to Hong Kong, Jean had been working for the Erskine family in Foster Gardens in Gosport, and was living- in as a domestic-cum-nanny. One evening, after visiting Mum, Dad and my sister Pat, she was cycling back to Gosport along Browndown Road in the dark when she fell off her bike. It was a badly lit area and the road was in a very poor state of repair with lots of pot-holes. As Jean's bike had large wheels and heavy frame, she could very easily have been really badly hurt. Nonetheless, it was very painful for her and she was badly shaken-up.

When Dad heard about her falling off the bike he said: '*That's it! She can come and live here and then she will only have to cycle in daylight.*' That was how Jean came to sleep in my bed. I was away, and what had been my bed was moved into Pat's room, and it became Pat and Jean's room. So, for more than a year before I returned home, Jean had been living with my parents and sister. By the time I arrived home, they were already just like a mum, dad and sister to her. For Jean, this was the first time that she could remember feeling part of a real family. Effectively she had lost contact with all of her birth family. When I came home, Jean had to keep to sleeping in the room with my sister for the three weeks before the wedding. That was a very long three weeks!

During those three weeks, I heard all about what had been happening in my absence. The first escapade involved the time when Jean and Pat went to the Coronation Ball at Lee Tower. Pat had been given free tickets at the Quick Turnover greengrocer's shop where she worked. It was the custom for the organisers of events which involved a large number of young servicemen, to give free tickets to young women in the local area, to balance up the numbers. Well, like Cinderella, they went to the ball. They said that in the ballroom there had been many American sailors, and practically every one they danced with asked if they could take them home after the dance. I understand that it ended up with them saying OK to quite a few of the sailors, just to stop them from asking. Shortly before the end of the ball, Pat said to Jean: '*We had better make a fast getaway,*' so they quickly got their coats and did a runner, with more than half a dozen American sailors in pursuit, each calling out '*You said I could take you home.*' Pat and Jean ran all the way down the High Street to the east end and hid in the doorway of the last shop, which was the 'Bazaar', a small sweet shop. Although I have sympathy with the young sailors, I am rather pleased that Jean and Pat did a runner. You know what sailors are! Well I do – I was one.

Pat and Rob had become engaged just after Pat's seventeenth birthday in September 1953 but after about six months it had

Jean on her bike at No 24

become a bit of an on-off arrangement, so much so that in the summer of 1954, Pat and Jean started going out as a foursome with Reg and Tony, a couple of chaps from Gosport. They went out two or three times, but Mum and Dad were not pleased when the two young men called at the house. In fact Mum and Dad were not keen on either of them. But it didn't last. After a visit to the cinema, Tony walked

Jean back to where she worked, because she was house-sitting for the family who going to be out until quite late. At the house things became a bit too serious, so the next time that Jean had a half-day she cycled to his home and told him that she wouldn't be seeing him again. Pat also packed up Reg.

In the Christmas period of 1954 it was all to change. One evening when Mum and Dad were out, Pat was in bed with the flu, and Jean was 'sister- sitting'. There was a knock on the door. Jean went downstairs to see who it was. She went back to Pat and said: '*You'll never guess who it is. IT'S THAT ROB.*' They were back together. Shortly after this, wedding plans began to be made. When I learnt that Pat and Rob were getting married, I wrote to the family and suggested that we should make it a double wedding. And that is how it came about. Nineteen days after I arrived home, Jean and I were married in a double wedding ceremony with Pat and Rob.

34

MARRIED AT LAST

On 18 June 1955 my sister, my new brother-in-law, my bride Jean and I held our wedding reception in the restaurant in Lee Tower. At our double wedding at St John the Evangelist in South Place, Herb Cottrill had given Jean away, and Brian Cottrill had been my best man. Once again Lee Tower was centre stage in our lives.

Our wedding

So in the few short years since doing the most stupid thing in my life, I moved on to doing the smartest thing that I have ever done.

After we were married, we lived at Anglesea Road. Like many other newlywed couples at that time, we lived with Mum and Dad, and it worked so well that we continued to live with them for the next eight years. In Anglesea Road, Jean and I had the upstairs. One bedroom was converted into a kitchen, another into a lounge; and Mum and Dad had the downstairs. We all shared the upstairs bathroom.

Pat moved out and she and Rob lived with his mum and dad in Gosport. After we returned from our honeymoon on the Isle of Wight, I joined a different radio company – IMR – and was appointed as Second Radio Officer on the *Samaria*. This was a Cunard passenger ship which travelled to and fro between Southampton or Liverpool and Quebec.

I missed the Bank Holiday at home, which by all accounts was a scorcher. Jean came to see me off at Southampton – she had intended it to be a surprise, and hadn't let me know that she was coming, but unfortunately I was ashore at the time, at the IMR office. When I came back to the ship she was waiting for me at the bottom of the gangway in the hot sun. The hot spell had started a bit before the Bank Holiday (then at the beginning of August), and it was reported in the press that *'the August Bank Holiday weekend was almost too hot with hundreds of cars lining the cliff lands. Lee became a boom town.'* It also reported that many were treated for cut feet by the St John's Ambulance Brigade. When I read this I wondered if those who had to be treated had paddled on the mussel beds near the pier.

The trip to Quebec was different to most of those I had become accustomed to. The food was of a similar standard to that on the *Corfu*; I even had my own table to which several passengers were allotted. I was not particularly impressed by Quebec, but I did managed one trip ashore on one afternoon. On the voyage back, as we were approaching the mouth of the St Lawrence, the ship's radar failed. I was not on watch, but the chief called on me to fix it. I had the distinct impression that the other radio officers on the ship were not up to dealing with the radar because at that time it didn't form part of many radio officer courses. I was able to fall back on some of my RAF training. By a careful process of elimination, I was able to find the fault, and fortunately the ship carried spares that enabled me to rectify the problem. After about a quarter of an hour I managed to get the radar working. Almost immediately a handful of icebergs appeared on the screen. They soon became visible to the lookout, and the ship changed course slightly in order not to get too close to them. As we passed by, I noticed some seals on one of them. I was surprised to discover that the icebergs had a smell, even the ones without seals.

After the ship returned from Quebec, there was a short interval of leave before I had to return back on board. When I did go back to the ship, I was told that I had been replaced. I was told this by my replacement. He was sleeping in what had been my bunk. From then on, I have always sympathised with the three bears and not Goldilocks. I was instructed to go home and await my next ship.

It was during this period of leave that I had a bit of a 'blast from the past' encounter. I was walking along the High Street in Lee-on-the-Solent, when who should I see walking towards me, with a young lady on his arm? None other than the then Third Officer, now Second Mate, that I had last seen when we went to the cinema and elsewhere in Bombay. He introduced me to his wife and said that they were on their honeymoon, staying at a bed-and-breakfast in Portsmouth Road, which was just around the corner from where we lived. Then I (unthinking) said '*I haven't seen you since Bombay when we went to ...*' the look of horror that came over his face turned to one of relief when I completed the sentence '*...the cinema.*' This encounter was, as in the name of the film, brief. I congratulated them both and told them that I had married my long-term girlfriend earlier that year. The conversation was soon cut short, after a few of those embarrassing silences that occur when those involved don't know what to say next, in case they say the wrong thing. We wished each other the best and said cheerio. I often wondered after that, why they had chosen Lee-on-the-Solent for their honeymoon.

35
FINISHED WITH THE SEA

Three weeks later I received a telegram telling me to go to Rotterdam to join a tanker. With memories of being 'shanghaied' in Hong Kong, I sent in my resignation, and decided to leave the Merchant Navy.

Three weeks after that, at the end of September, I got a job with Ultra, a radio and television manufacturing company that was setting up in Gosport. Initially Ultra had a pilot factory in the Hall, a large three-storey Victorian building in Trinity Green, Gosport. It was situated between Trinity Church and the harbour, roughly where the car park of Seaward Tower is now located. I was the third local male employee to be taken on. Being so close to the waterfront, it was possible to take lunchtime walks near the Gosport Ferry, and keep abreast of what was going on in the harbour.

As well as the changes that had been taking place in Lee-on-the-Solent and the local area, and in my life, this was also a time of greater changes in the wider world. After the end of World War II, the long-hoped-for time of peace seemed to be elusive. The demise of the British Empire had begun and the world had entered a phase of non-combatant mutual animosity with the 'Cold War'. It had started just before I joined the RAF, and the Soviets had turned the temperature down a notch or two by trying to isolate Berlin, which had been thwarted by the Berlin Airlift. Here we were seven years later: relations between the West and the USSR, although still frosty, had stabilised and had possibly improved a little. Living in this period was a bit like living with the sword of Damocles continually hanging over us, and many people secretly worried about the future. The balance of mutual destruction between the two great powers meant that a home with a nuclear bunker was a sought-after des res, and it was claimed by someone known to Rob's mum, that they had been involved in the construction of a deep nuclear bunker, for the Royal Family and some of the Government, near Devizes. Nevertheless, the underlying fear did have an impact on the 'attitude to life' of many.

In the April of 1956 there was a 'goodwill visit' paid by the Russian leaders Marshal Bulganin and Mr Krushchev. They were aboard the cruiser *Ordzhonikdze* which, for the duration of the visit, was anchored in Portsmouth Harbour. I saw it several times during my lunchtime walks. It was easy to tell that it was 'a stranger in town'. Apart from the flag flying at the stern, the ship was painted a different grey to that of RN vessels, and it had different 'lines' with a sharper 'fluted' bow. There was an incident concerning this warship which came to light later that had some far-reaching consequences. A Commander Lionel 'Buster' Crabb, who was a James Bond-like character, apparently, disappeared while this visit was taking place. It was believed that he had been carrying out some underwater spying mission. The only fact that appears to have any certainty is that, just over a year later, a headless, handless body in underwater clothing was discovered in Chichester Harbour. Which may, or may not, have been him. One account states that Buster Crabb entered the water at Forton to swim to the Soviet ship. As relations with the USSR went into the freezer big-time after this incident, with hindsight we may conclude that Gosport was a significant location, in the deterioration of relations in the Cold War at that time.

A couple of months before these mysterious 'goings on' in Portsmouth Harbour, Jean discovered she was pregnant. Most of the ladies in the church congregation came to the correct conclusion about her condition when she fainted in church. Only a few weeks before this, there had been an appeal on the radio for Jean Burtoo to urgently contact the police, as her mother was dangerously ill in hospital and had asked to see her. Actually we didn't hear the message ourselves – someone must have given our address to the police, because they came to the house to inform us. We went to St Richard's Hospital at Chichester, where Jean saw her mother for the first time in five years. Her mother was dying. This was the first and only time that I saw my mother-in-law.

Over the next few years we did try to maintain some contact with Jean's family, but it was not very successful. She, through no fault of her own, had become an outsider in that family. But she had become a treasured member of her new family, and she was soon to become the 'heart' of a new family within the family.

36

BEST-DRESSED IN THE MESS

With the prospect of starting a family, my thoughts became focused on how best to provide for them, and after comparing the money that I was earning with what I had earned when I was at sea, I decided to give the Merchant Navy another try. So in May 1956 I left Ultra and rejoined Marconi. It may have been the extra money, or it may have been that I was suffering from a bit of 'nautical indigestion'. Maybe I hadn't swallowed the anchor properly. So I donned the uniform again. This time no luxury liner, not even a cargo ship, and thankfully not a 'tramp ship'. I ended up on a small tanker, the *Saguaro*, which had the big advantage that, at that time, she was based in Fawley.

I was new to tankers. When I went to the mess for my first meal, as it was summer, I had on a pair of white shorts, a white shirt with epaulettes, white socks and shoes. When I entered the mess, all heads turned. Being a 'head turner' was not a good thing. They say that first impressions count. I think the impression of those sat around the table would have been … 'What a prat'. I looked around; the way that I could best describe their attire was that they looked as if they had just come from a building site – another case of 'one of life's Ooops!' It did mean that I had a bit of a problem, because nearly all of my gear was that type of uniform. I certainly didn't have any jeans or check shirts. When I returned to my cabin I took off my epaulettes and changed the white shoes for black ones, and that was about the best that I could do.

The voyage out was uneventful: straight to the end of the 'Med' to Banias in Syria, where I became aware of why the dress code on board was so relaxed – the crew never went anywhere, the ship was a little closed world. We anchored about four miles off Banias, adjacent to a cylindrical buoy, which was a bit like an oversized oil-drum, attached to which was a flexible oil pipeline. This pipeline was duly hauled aboard and connected to one of the ship's tanks. Shortly after, we started having our cargo pumped on board. Loading only took a matter of hours. It seemed as if in no time at all we were finished with our self- service filling station, the pipeline was disconnected, we weighed anchor, and set off on our return journey. When the *Saguaro* arrived back in the Solent, she was anchored off Cowes. The Captain, knowing that I was soon to become a father, allowed me to go ashore with the Customs men in their boat into Cowes. He knew that the tanker would only be at Fawley for two days before she would be off again.

Although the *Saguaro* was at anchor less than four miles from Lee Tower, it took me nearly three hours to get home. After I left the Customs boat, I had to get a bus from Cowes to Newport, then a bus to Ryde, a ferry to Portsmouth, a ferry to Gosport and finally a bus to Lee. The Customs officers in the launch had helped me with my small holdall that contained my dirty washing, at least that is what I had told them. Actually it had in it twice the cigarette allowance, which was for my Dad, padded out with a little dirty washing.

When I arrived home and saw Jean at the top of the stairs waiting for me, heavily pregnant, smiling with the radiance that only pregnant women have, the tortuous journey home had all been worthwhile. I can still picture the green maternity wrap-round skirt that she was wearing. At that moment I dreaded the thought of going back to the ship; I wanted to be here with her.

The next trip was to Ras Tanura in the Persian Gulf (its name means Oven Cape and is well named). This run finally confirmed my feelings that a life at sea was not for me, so when we arrived back at Fawley just over three weeks later, as it could possibly my last chance of signing off for some while (because it had to be done in a British home port) I signed off.

Less than four weeks later our daughter Susan was born, and I resigned from Marconi's a week after that. This time I had been at sea for less than three months, but being with Jean and our new baby was far more important to me than the extra money. Nevertheless in those days it was important to have a job; it was almost a case of no job, no money. The day after resigning from Marconi, I went to the Labour Exchange and got a job as a labourer on one of the machines in the Ashley Wallpaper factory in Gosport. As I had become a father, with all of the ensuing financial responsibilities, I never had to be asked twice if I wanted to do overtime, but as it happened, I had to work as a labourer only for three weeks. I was fortunate enough to be able to rejoin Ultra, at their new factory on Fareham Road, Gosport.

I HAD SWALLOWED THE ANCHOR FOR GOOD.

No more lonely sea and the sky for me.

Now we are a family

37

A TIT-BIT

My birth certificate shows that I was born on 17 November 1931 at RAF Hospital Cranwell, in Cranwell and Byard's Leap in Lincolnshire, and that my Dad was an LAC (leading aircraftsman) in the RAF.

Who was Byard, you may ask? It was not a who but a what; it was in fact a blind horse in local folklore (though Byard appears in a number of continental medieval legends too). According to the legend, sometime in the past there was an evil witch who lived in the area in a cave or hut. I think a cave might be somewhat unlikely in an area that is as flat as a pancake. Nevertheless, in the true tradition of witch stories, she was responsible for most of the misfortunes that befell the local inhabitants including withering crops. The locals enlisted the help of a retired soldier who stated that he would kill the witch by driving his sword through the heart of 'old Meg' as she was known. For some reason he decided that he needed a horse with fast reactions, possibly so that he could beat a hasty retreat before she could turn him into a frog or something similar if things got out of hand. To select a suitable horse, he went to a pond where some horses were drinking and threw a stone into the pond and the horse that reacted quickest was a blind horse known as 'Blind Byard' which was the one he chose.

Mounting Byard, he set out for old Meg's lair and called her out, but somehow she managed to outwit him and managed to creep up behind his horse and jabbed her long nails into its rear, scaring the living daylights out of the animal. Byard leapt over 60 feet (that is more than twice the men's world long-jump record) and ran off with the ex-soldier astride and the old witch in pursuit. However, when they reached the pond the hero of the story regained control of the horse, turned round and thrust his sword through the heart of old Meg. She fell into the pond and drowned. The spot where Byard is supposed to have landed in his remarkable leap is marked (for tourists?) by a small bordered patch in the ground with four horseshoe imprints. (They look rather close together).

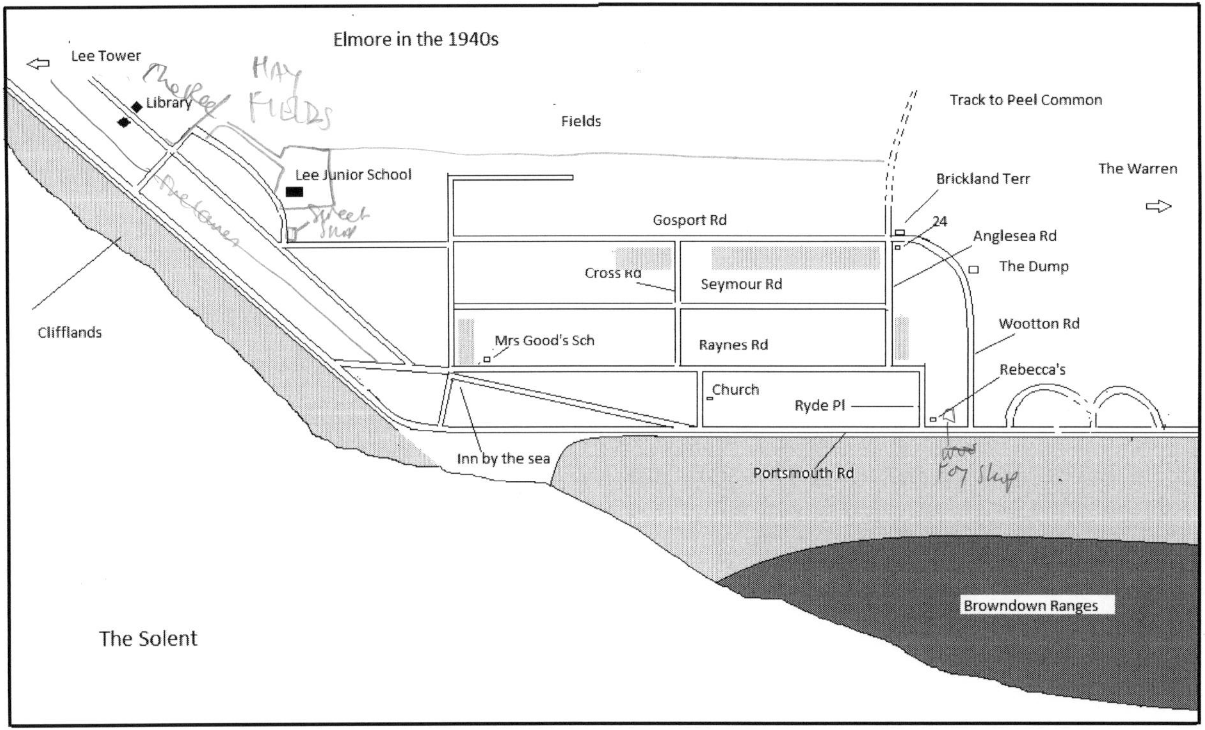

Map of Elmore during the 1940s

ACKNOWLEDGEMENTS

I would like to extend my thanks to Amanda Field of Chaplin Books for her guiding hand in the gestation period and delivery of this book.